# Nickel Quilts

## Great Designs from 5-Inch Scraps

## Pat Speth and
## Charlene Thode

Nickel Quilts: Great Designs from 5-Inch Scraps
© 2002 by Pat Speth and Charlene Thode

That Patchwork Place®
is an imprint of Martingale & Company™.

20205 144th Avenue NE
Woodinville, WA 98072-8478
www.martingale-pub.com

Printed in Hong Kong
07 06 05 04 03 02          8 7 6 5 4 3 2 1

Library of Congress Cataloging-in-Publication Data
Speth, Pat.
   Nickel quilts / Pat Speth and Charlene Thode.
      p. cm.
   ISBN 1-56477-416-3
      1. Patchwork—Patterns. 2. Quilting—Patterns.
   I. Thode, Charlene. II. Title.

TT835 .S6377 2002
746.46'041—dc21

                                        2001057903

### Credits

President ❖ Nancy J. Martin
CEO ❖ Daniel J. Martin
Publisher ❖ Jane Hamada
Editorial Director ❖ Mary V. Green
Managing Editor ❖ Tina Cook
Technical Editor ❖ Barbara Weiland
Copy Editor ❖ Karen Koll
Design Director ❖ Stan Green
Illustrator ❖ Laurel Strand
Text Designer ❖ Regina Girard
Cover Designer ❖ Stan Green
Photographer ❖ Brent Kane

### Mission Statement

*We are dedicated to providing quality products and service by working together to inspire creativity and to enrich the lives we touch.*

## Dedication

To our children: Ray, Roxie, Matt, Michelle, and Mike.
Thanks for being such wonderful kids.

## Acknowledgments

We'd like to thank our families for being so flexible and
extremely understanding during all the communal meals we
served while we worked on this book. Thanks for letting us turn
our houses into quilting studios and for all your extra help, too.

We'd also like to thank the members of the Mississippi
Valley Quilt Guild and our fellow "retreaters" for their
encouragement and support.

Thanks to Robin Korth for making three of the
quilts for the book.

And last, we'd like to thank Martingale and Company
for helping us realize our dream.

# ❧ *Contents* ❧

Why Nickel Quilts?                               7

How to Gather 5" Squares                         8
  *Start Cutting*                                8
  *A Few Trading Guidelines*                     8
  *What about Other Sizes?*                      9

General Directions                              10
  *Taking Stock of Your Sewing Tools*           10
  *Selecting Fabric and Thread*                 11
  *Preparing the Fabric*                        11
  *Cutting the Strips and Squares*              12
  *Sewing, Pinning, and Marking*                13
  *Constructing and Pressing Units*             14

Finishing Your Quilt                           21
  *Assembling the Quilt Top*                    21
  *Adding the Borders*                          21
  *Marking the Quilt Top for Quilting*          22
  *Making the Quilt Backing*                    22
  *Layering, Basting, and Quilting*             23
  *Adding the Binding*                          24
  *Labeling Your Quilt*                         25

The Quilt Patterns 27

    *Jewel Box* 28

    *Autumn Stretched Star* 31

    *Sunny Lanes* 34

    *Northern Lights* 38

    *Four-Patch Plaid* 42

    *Millennium Star* 46

    *Paducah Nine Patch* 50

    *Mount Hood* 54

    *Tillie's Treasure* 58

    *Shaded Four Patch* 62

    *Morning Star* 66

    *Flying Home from Bali Bali* 70

    *Pinwheel* 74

    *Labor Day Madness* 78

    *Ozark Maple Leaf* 82

    *Buffalo Ridge* 87

    *Dutchman's Puzzle* 91

    *All That Glitters* 96

    *Big Dipper* 101

    *Arlington Square* 106

Glossary 111

About the Authors 112

# ❧ Why Nickel Quilts? ❧

We love scrappy quilts, and our method for making them is fast, easy, and promises very accurate piecing—if you follow our advice for stitching. You'll begin with a collection of "nickel squares." What's that? A nickel square is a 5" square of quilting fabric. You'll need lots of them to make a scrappy nickel quilt. Since gathering fabrics for a nickel quilt can take time, we have developed a method for building your nickel-square stash quickly through fabric trades with friends, new and old, who share your love for quilting.

Each of the quilt patterns in this book is rated by skill level—easy, beginner, or intermediate—based on the degree of piecing difficulty. If you're new to quilting, start with a "beginner" quilt. If you have some quilting experience, choose an "easy" project. Once you've used our easy unit-construction methods to make your first nickel quilt, you'll be ready to move on to one of the more challenging projects.

You will use combinations of eight different units to create the blocks used in the quilts featured in this book. The directions for making the units begin on page 14. Our simple method of sewing and dividing a 5" square into the pieced units practically eliminates the need for complicated math (aka work). To really understand our methods, *it is essential to review the unit construction steps for each unit before you begin.* It is also important to make a sample block or blocks for the quilt you are making.

Before you know it, you'll be hooked on this easy way to make scrappy quilts—but don't blame us if somehow all of the fabric in your stash gets cut into 5" squares.

Happy stitching to all, and may your points always match!

Pat and Charlene

# How to Gather 5″ Squares

Let's face it, making a scrappy quilt is a lot like going to a potluck dinner or an all-you-can-eat buffet; you can have a little of a lot of different things instead of that plain tuna casserole you were going to eat at home! Having only a few different fabrics in your fabric stash is just not much fun, wouldn't you agree? If you're anything at all like the two of us, what you really want is to walk into a quilt shop and say, "I'll take a yard of everything!" Since that's a nice fantasy, but a little unrealistic, you need an easy, inexpensive way to gather enough different fabrics to make truly scrappy nickel quilts. It's easier than you think. Collecting enough 5″ squares for your nickel quilt is part of the fun of making it.

## Start Cutting

So, how do you start collecting all those 5″ squares? Start by cutting strips from your own fabric collection. When fabric shopping, always buy a little more than you need for your project so you can cut a 5″-wide strip from each one—after you've tested it for colorfastness, preshrunk it, and trimmed away the selvages. Cut each strip into squares and store for future use. You'll be surprised how quickly your pile grows with your fabric purchases alone.

Want to make the variety in your collection of squares grow even more quickly? Plan a cutting bee with a few friends and swap strips. In addition, many quilt shops and mail-order catalogs offer packets of 5″ squares. Don't forget to check out all those new Internet fabric shopping sites, too. Not only can you buy fabric packets online, but there are also dozens of online lists of quilters interested in fabric trades. Fat-quarter trades are wonderful. Did you know you can cut twelve 5″ squares from one fat quarter? Use some for your current scrap project and put the leftovers away for good measure!

If you aren't able to access the Internet, look through your quilting magazines for letters from quilters who want to participate in fabric trades—or you can write a letter yourself, asking for trading partners. When you trade with others from different states and other countries, your selection of squares becomes that much more varied and unique. If staying a bit closer to home is more your style, then start a trade with your local quilt guild or your smaller "sit-and-sew" group.

## A Few Trading Guidelines

You may find it helpful to organize your fabric trade with a few guiding principles. Begin by drafting a friend or two to help out.

- Select the type(s) of fabric the group would like to trade. For example, you could begin by designating a different color for each month, or a different type of print, such as stripes, stars, paisleys, florals, or plaids. Or, you could decide to swap fabrics that represent specific time periods—1800 or 1930 reproduction fabrics, for example. Some swappers even go so far as to designate the manufacturers whose fabric they want to swap.

- Decide how many times per year you want to trade. If you're trading with guild members, it's a good idea to schedule six trades per year so you can have the participants drop off packets one month and pick them up the next. Midway between your regular meetings, get your small group of volunteers together to organize the fabric into sets for pick up. Those who may have missed the drop-off meeting can still participate at that time if they want to drop off their fabric.

- Determine how many squares you're going to trade. That will depend a lot on the size of your group. You may want to ask people to sign up first to get an idea of the number of participants you'll have. Be sure to let them know that they can submit multiple trades. As an example, in our guild each person brings for one trade 144 squares, or 72 pairs, and as long as there are at least 72 trades turned in, no one receives any duplicates. We've also discovered that trading the 5″ squares of fabric in pairs makes it easier to create a wider range of blocks and frees up the design elements of your quilts. Just like the animals on the ark, trade those squares two by two.

(Big confession: We both submit at least four or five trades per month. We may not be the official winners of the "whoever dies with the most fabric wins" contest—yet—but if the two of us pooled our fabric collections, we'd be awfully close! You might say our fabric stashes border on the obscene!)

- Make sure everyone understands that *all fabrics must be 100 percent cotton* and that they must be *preshrunk and tested for colorfastness* before the swap. Selvages should be removed *before* you cut the strips.

## ✦ Nickel Tip ✦

Save those old mismatched white socks with the holes in them! Just throw one in along with your fabric (especially the dark colors and reds) when you wash it, and you'll know whether you have a bleeder or renegade in the mix. There's nothing sadder than putting together a wonderful quilt and *then* having a fabric bleed.

- Remind all participants that you get as good as you give. Depending on who is involved, the fabrics you receive might not be ones you would have personally selected—but that's what makes scrap quilts so interesting. Remind participants to be kind and to use this as a learning experience.

- Ask participants to stack their trade in twos, staggering each pair of 5" squares, and place them in a gallon-size plastic bag with their name on the outside. This will make things go faster when it's time to actually swap the fabric squares.

- Plan a party! Pick a day to get together and trade the fabrics. Think about having a potluck lunch or dessert party. Most important, have *fun*. Remember, anyone who comes to help with the swap gets to fondle the fabric first! It's nice to have a large space for setting out the trades. Ping-Pong tables are great. Count the number of trades turned in and mark that number on the table with slips of paper. Beginning at one end, place one pair of fabrics on each slip of paper. When the first stack runs out, start on the next stack and keep going until all of the fabrics have been traded. Place one traded stack back into each reusable bag to take back to the next meeting. Depending on the number of participants, you may get some of your own fabric back.

Once you have a wonderful stack of 5" squares, half the work—the cutting—is already done! Just select the squares for your blocks and start sewing. We know that once you see what a big time-saver this method is, you'll be wishing you'd started trading a long time ago.

---

**5"-Square Yardage Yield**
*(based on 40" of usable width after preshrinking)*

¼ yd. = 8 squares

1 fat quarter = 12 squares

½ yd. = 24 squares

¾ yd. = 40 squares

1 yd. = 56 squares

---

## What about Other Sizes?

If you have been trading something other than 5" squares, don't worry. The alternate square chart below gives the unfinished size for the various units you'll need to make the quilts in this book. You can follow the same methods in the unit-construction section but just be aware that since the block size will be different, the measurements in the illustrations will not match your unit measurements. You will also need to recalculate the yardage for sashings, borders, and backing when you substitute squares of a different size.

| | 4" square | 5" square | 6" square |
|---|---|---|---|
| Two-patch unit | 3½" | 4½" x 5" | 5½" x 6" |
| Four-patch unit | 3½" | 4½" | 5½" |
| Half-square-triangle unit | 3½" | 4½" | 5½" |
| Small-wonders unit | 3" | 4" | 5" |
| Combination unit | 3¼" | 4¼" | 5¼" |
| Hourglass unit | 3" | 4" | 5" |
| Picket-fence unit | 3½" | 4½" | 5½" |
| Flying-geese unit | 2 x 3½" | 2½" x 4½" | 3" x 5½" |

# ❦ General Directions ❧

## Taking Stock of Your Sewing Tools

Before you start your first nickel quilt, make sure you have the following basic tools:

**B.S.K. (that's Basic Sewing Kit):** Our B.S.K. consists of thread, a small pair of scissors, a tool to help guide the fabric under the presser foot (perhaps a seam ripper or stilletto), pins, needles, measuring tape, bandages (for the occasional rotary-cutting accident), a mechanical pencil and a small notebook for making notes and keeping track of all the new ideas that float into our heads while we're sewing, a seam ripper (dare we even say that?), and most important—chocolate! We never do anything or leave the house without it!

**Design wall:** You'll need—and want—a design wall. Our design walls are portable and fit into our cars so we can take them along to retreats and workshops. See the box at right to make your own portable design wall.

**Iron and ironing surface:** You can use a tabletop ironing surface when constructing and pressing the units, but you will definitely need a full-size ironing board or other large pressing surface as your quilt grows and you add the borders.

**Rotary cutter and mat:** We work with two sizes of mats—one large enough to accommodate the fabric when folded in half with selvages aligned and a smaller mat to keep next to the sewing machine for trimming the pieced units during construction. We prefer the mats marked with grid lines. We also prefer a *sharp* rotary cutter with a blade that is at least 2" in diameter. To avoid frustration, don't put off changing the blade when it dulls or develops "skips" when cutting. Using a dull blade doubles your work, and quiltmaking is about having *fun*, not about getting frustrated with your cutter!

**Rulers:** You'll need a square ruler, 6" or larger, with a 45° angle marked and a 6" x 24" rotary ruler for cutting. You can get by with a 6" x 12" ruler, but you will need to double-fold your fabrics prior to cutting the strips.

---

### Portable Design Wall

In less than 5 minutes and with only a few easy-to-find materials, you can make an inexpensive and portable design wall that you can take anywhere and that doesn't take a lot of storage space when not in use.

- 1 dressmaker's cardboard cutting board (the kind that folds up for storage)
- 2 strips of 1" x 2" wood, each at least 5' long; they can be longer, but just be sure they will fit in your vehicle and aren't taller than your sewing-room ceilings)
- A flannel-backed vinyl tablecloth or a 40" x 72" piece of white flannel
- 6 large binder clips (from the office-supply store)

1. Unfold the cutting board and place it on a flat surface.
2. Place the wood strips underneath along the long edges of the cutting board, making sure they are even across the bottom so the design wall sits squarely on the floor.
3. Lay the tablecloth (flannel side up) or the piece of flannel on top of the cutting board and fasten the three layers—wood, cutting board, and flannel—together with binder clips. Use three on each long edge.

---

**Sewing machine:** Make sure your sewing machine is in good working order! Give it a good cleaning and put in a new needle. We recommend changing the machine needle at the beginning of a new project, or after approximately ten to fifteen hours of actual sewing time.

## Selecting Fabric and Thread

Now for the fabric fondling! We recommend buying good-quality, 100 percent–cotton fabrics and thread. Match the weight of the thread to the fabrics. Using a heavy thread on a lightweight fabric causes additional wear and tear in the fabric along the stitching lines and will shorten the life of your quilt.

We recommend a neutral color thread for piecing scrap quilts. Tan, gray, and off-white are all good choices because they blend with the wide variety of colors in the varied fabrics you'll be using in your scrap quilt. We also recommend using the same kind of thread on top and in the bobbin for piecing and for quilting. We've found this strategy prevents a lot of sewing machine "tension" headaches.

Many of the quilts in this book have a very definite "theme" reflected in the colors and fabrics we chose, but we've found that just about anything goes in scrap quilts. Choose colors to suit your taste. Emphasize color value and vary the size of print motifs in the fabric assortment for a quilt.

### The Value of Value

Because the quilts in this book are all scrappy and each is made from lots of different fabrics, it's more important to pay attention to the value of the fabrics (whether they are light, medium, or dark) than it is to worry about how they relate to each other on the color wheel. If you plan the placement of dark-, medium-, and light-colored fabrics correctly within the blocks and distribute evenly the various colors you've used throughout the quilt top, you'll achieve the same effect without obsessing about it.

If you're confused about whether a fabric is dark, medium, or light, try separating your fabrics into a dark pile and a light pile. You'll soon realize that you have a few that aren't either one; those are the mediums. Just be aware that a medium fabric can look dark next to a white fabric or a light tone-on-tone print but light next to a very dark blue or black fabric.

For an inexpensive value finder, purchase a red plastic report cover (available at your local office-supply store) and view your fabrics through it. You won't be able to see the actual colors of the fabric through the red plastic—just the values. Test this technique with fabrics from your scrap bag. Experimenting is the best way to learn.

**Note:** The red-plastic value finder does not work with red fabrics, but if you get proficient at identifying value in other colors, you'll find it fairly easy to judge red values, too.

### The Value of Variety

When choosing fabrics for a scrap quilt, it's important to vary the size of the prints, stripes, or plaids. Be sure you mix in large floral prints with small geometrics and large plaids with stripes. Throw in a few holiday or other seasonal fabrics as well. We also recommend using a variety of background fabrics in the blocks rather than just one. It adds more interest and movement to the finished quilt.

We've actually used fabric wrong side up in a few quilts, because the value and contrast were what we needed. (You've probably done this accidentally a time or two, during nighttime quilting sessions when the lighting wasn't so good. Right?) Remember, you aren't dressing yourself; you're making a quilt; you *can* use the wrong side if it suits your purpose.

## Preparing the Fabric

We both definitely recommend prewashing *all* fabrics, and insist that this be one of the rules in any fabric trade. Using prewashed fabrics helps reduce the likelihood of having a fabric bleed or run later and ruin all your hard work. In addition, a quilt top made with both washed and unwashed fabrics is more likely to shrink unevenly, leaving unsightly puckers in the laundered quilt.

Although we agree that fabrics should be prewashed, we each have our own method. One of us washes in clear water, the other in water with a mild laundry detergent (partially because a little dirty laundry usually gets thrown in along with the fabric). Don't forget our old-sock theory. Throw one in along with your fabrics; if it changes color in the wash, there's a renegade fabric in the batch. Red fabrics are particularly notorious for bleeding and turning the sock a pale pink! Navy and black are other common bleeders.

To prevent wrinkles from setting, avoid letting your fabrics sit in the dryer for any great length of time after they are dry. Wrinkles make ironing the fabrics a real job.

Take note that this is the only time you will hear us recommend "ironing" the fabric. Once you cut the fabric and begin the block construction, you will only "press." There's a huge difference. Ironing is work. It requires effort to push the iron back and forth across the fabric to remove wrinkles. When you press during construction, you lift, place, and press down lightly on the iron, rather than moving it back and forth. Ironing, as opposed to pressing, causes distortion in your quilt blocks. Let the weight of the iron do the work for you when you press.

After you've completed your quilt, we recommend that you wash it with a very mild soap or one developed specifically for cleaning quilts. We both use Orvus paste to launder our finished quilts. It's inexpensive, safe, and lasts a long time.

## Cutting the Strips and Squares

After you've prepared your fabric, it's time to cut it into strips and squares. Choose your fabric squares and make a sample block before cutting all of the fabrics for your quilt project. You will learn and practice the steps required to make the block, which will allow you to speed up the piecing. You can also check and adjust color and value placement if necessary.

1. Straighten the fabric. Hold it in front of you with the selvages aligned and examine the fold. If there are waves or wrinkles along the folded edge, realign the selvages to the right or left until the fold is hanging evenly. Don't worry about the cut edges (crosswise grain) of the fabric. Even if you've torn the fabric instead of cutting it, this edge may still be off when you align the selvages so that *the folded edge is smooth and flat*. Place the fabric on the cutting mat with the folded edge along one of the grid lines on the mat.

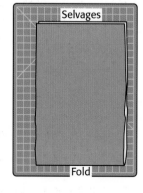

2. To make the first cut, place the ruler along the folded edge and align a crosswise line with the fold. Cut the strip slightly wider than the actual size you need. For example, if you need a 5"-wide strip, be sure to cut it at least 5½" wide to begin. Hold the rotary cutter against the ruler and cut alongside it, moving the cutter away from your body. Stop and move the hand that's holding the ruler as needed to keep it from slipping out of position.

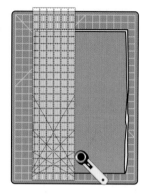

3. Turn the entire mat around and trim the strip to the correct width. Try not to disturb the rest of the fabric during this process. Cut as many strips as needed from each fabric.

4. Cut the strips into squares. Use our trick to make fast work of this when you've cut several strips. Position a fabric strip on the mat with one long edge along one of the horizontal grid lines. Align the selvage edge with a vertical grid line. Place the next strip of fabric on top of the first one, but move it up one grid line. The selvages of the second strip should be along the same grid line as the first strip. Continue to layer up to five strips of fabric in this way. (To ensure accurate cuts, don't try to layer more than five.)

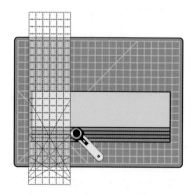

Layer strips before cutting squares.

5. Make the first cut as you did when cutting the strips. Position the ruler on the fabric, aligning the markings along the top and bottom edges of the fabric strips. Make sure that the first cut allows for a wider strip than required so there is room to trim away the selvages. Putting pressure on both the ruler and the rotary cutter, make the first cut. Make sure the ruler is positioned so that the selvages will be completely removed from the layered strips in the first cut.

6. Turn the mat around, align the ruler at the top and bottom edges, and cut the strips into squares.

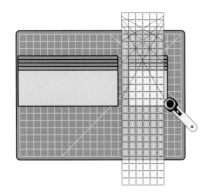

Trim selvages from first cut.

## Sewing, Pinning, and Marking

All quilts in this book are made using ¼" -wide seam allowances. If you have one for your machine, use the ¼" presser foot to stitch accurate seam widths. If not, measure ¼" from the point of the needle to the right and mark with a strip of masking tape on the bed of your machine. Or, use a piece of moleskin foam (a foot-care product, available at your local drug store). It's thicker than tape and creates a raised guide for the fabric edges while you are stitching.

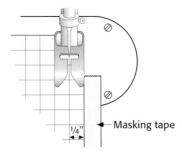

← Masking tape
¼"

### Chain Sewing

Chain sewing is a great way to save time and thread. Simply stitch two pieces together, stitch off the end of the pieces, and feed the next set of pieces under the foot without clipping the thread or lifting the presser

In some cases, we will tell you to use a "slim" ¼"-wide seam allowance. This means that you will stitch a slightly narrower seam so the stitching is a thread from the normal ¼" seam line. This allows for the thickness of the sewing thread in the seam allowance and actually results in a more accurately sized unit.

In other cases, you will be instructed to stitch a "very slim" ¼"-wide seam. We use a ³⁄₁₆"-wide seam allowance for this when it takes several seams to complete a unit—and again, it ensures that all units are accurate.

foot. This will also help keep the pieces in order when you join the rows in the blocks.

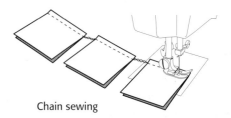

Chain sewing

### To Pin or Not to Pin

That is the question. It depends on you and your sewing machine. We recommend pinning when points need to be matched and whenever working with units that have seams in them. Pinning helps keep the seam allowances in place. We also pin when sewing on bias edges, and when joining the blocks and adding the borders. Use pins that have a fine shaft to avoid damaging the fabric. Fine pins also slide in and out of fabric more easily. We do have one firm rule: Don't ever sew over pins; remove them before you reach them to avoid snagged fabric, bent pins, broken needles, and possible injury.

### Marking

We recommend marking stitching lines *only* when making half-square-triangle and picket-fence units that require a diagonal sewing line. We've tried a variety of methods for making these units, but we prefer the one in this book as it gives us the most accurate results. Of course, you are free to use another method for these units if you prefer.

# Constructing and Pressing Units

The quilts in this book are made from combinations of eight different units: two-patch, four-patch, half-square-triangle, small-wonders, combination, hourglass, picket-fence, and flying-geese. Follow the directions shown below to construct the various units. Be sure to "set the seams" by placing the iron on the stitched seam line *before* pressing it to one side or the other. Remember: *press; do not iron.*

## Two-Patch Units

1. With right sides together, place a 5" square of the background fabric on a 5" square of the main fabric. Stitch ¼"-wide seams on opposite sides of the unit. Cut the unit in half so that each piece measures 2½" x 5".

Stitch ¼" seams
at opposite edges.

2. Press to set the stitching; then press the seam allowance toward the darker fabric in the unit.

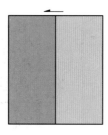

Press.

3. When the quilt directions call for "large two-patch units," trim ½" from one edge so the unit measures 4½" square.

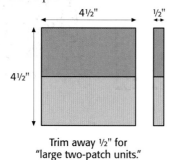

Trim away ½" for
"large two-patch units."

## Four-Patch Units

1. Follow steps 1–3 for the two-patch units.

2. With right sides together, seams aligned, and the *dark and light fabrics opposite each other,* stitch ¼" from opposite sides. Be sure stitching crosses the first seam. Cut the resulting unit in half.

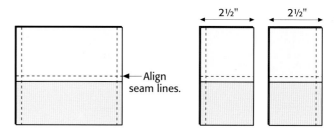

Align
seam lines.

3. Press to set the stitching; then press the seam to one side in each four-patch unit.

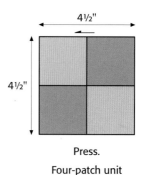

Press.
Four-patch unit

## Half-Square-Triangle Units

1. Draw a diagonal line on the wrong side of a 5" square of background fabric. With right sides together, place the marked background square on top of a square of the main fabric.

Wrong side of
background fabric

2. Stitch a "slim" ¼"-wide seam on both sides of the diagonal line (see box on page 13).

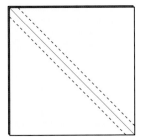

Stitch a "slim" ¼"
on each side of the line.

3. Cut along the diagonal line to yield 2 half-square-triangle units. Set the stitching by placing the iron on the seam line of each resulting unit for one second.

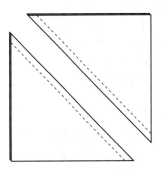

Cut on the diagonal line.

### Sew and Flip

Both the flying-geese and picket-fence units utilize the "sew-and-flip" method to add the small squares that become the triangular corners after trimming. *When adding these units, stitch one thread width to the outside of the diagonal line.* This stitching strategy allows for the thickness of the thread in the seam and results in a more accurately sized block after pressing.

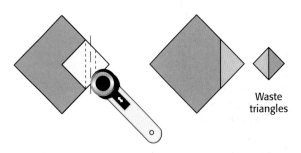

Waste triangles

Following are just a few examples of blocks made using only the waste triangles.

### Waste Triangles

Waste triangles are "bonus" half-square triangles that you can make when constructing picket-fence and flying-geese units, using the corners that are cut away. Sew the small squares in place as directed, and then stitch again ½" from the first line of stitching. You can "eyeball" this seam because you will trim these small half-square triangle units to the exact size you need when you use them in a future project.

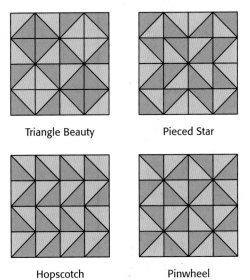

Triangle Beauty

Pieced Star

Hopscotch

Pinwheel

4. Press the seam in each unit toward the dark fabric, unless otherwise directed in the individual block illustrations for the quilt you are making.

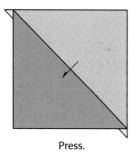

Press.

5. Place the 45° diagonal line of your square ruler along the seam line. Position so that the fabric extends past the ruler on 2 adjacent sides and the remaining sides extend past the 4½" lines on the ruler. Trim away the fabric that extends beyond the ruler edges.

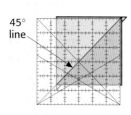

Trim excess.

6. Reposition the unit so that the 2 trimmed edges now line up along the 4½" lines on the ruler and the diagonal ruler line is along the seam line. Trim the remaining 2 edges for a perfect 4½" half-square-triangle unit.

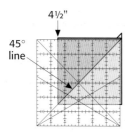

Trim excess.

Half-square-
triangle unit

## Small-Wonders Units

1. Follow steps 1–6 to make a half-square-triangle unit. Position the half-square-triangle unit as shown, with the dark triangle in the lower right-hand corner. Cut the unit in half.

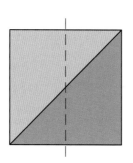
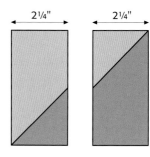

2. *Lift the ruler carefully* and reposition so the 2¼" line is along the lower edge of the unit. Cut along the upper edge of the ruler. You should have 4 different pieces, each one measuring 2¼".

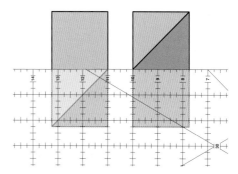

Position 2¼" line at lower edge of units.

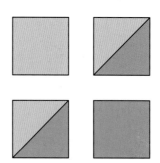

Small-wonders units
Each unit should measure 2¼" square.

## Combination Units

1. For this unit only, use a "very slim" ¼" seam allowance (see box on page 13) and follow steps 1–4 for half-square-triangle units on pages 14–16. *Do not trim the units.*

2. On the wrong side of the untrimmed half-square-triangle unit, draw a diagonal line perpendicular to the seam line.

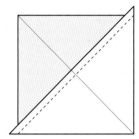

Untrimmed half-square-triangle unit

3. With right sides together, center the marked unit on top of a 5" square of fabric. (It will be slightly smaller than the 5" square.) Stitch a "very slim" seam on both sides of the diagonal line (see box on page 13).

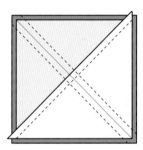

Stitch a "very slim" ¼" seam on each side of diagonal line.

4. Cut on the diagonal line. Set the stitching and press the seam toward the large triangle.

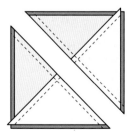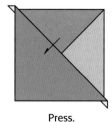

Press.

5. Align the 45° diagonal line of the square ruler with the long seam line in the unit. Position the ruler so that the fabric extends past the ruler on 2 adjacent edges, with the 2 remaining edges extending past the 4¼" lines of the ruler and with the 4¼" line meeting the short seam line on the unit. Trim away the fabric extending past the ruler.

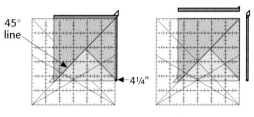

Trim excess.

6. Reposition the unit so that the 2 trimmed edges now line up with the 4¼" lines on the ruler and the 45° diagonal line of the ruler is aligned with the long seam line. Trim the remaining 2 edges. You should have a perfect, 4¼"-square combination unit.

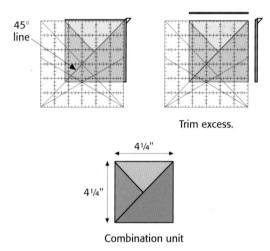

Trim excess.

Combination unit

## Hourglass Units

1. Follow only steps 1–4 for half-square triangles on pages 14–16. *Do not trim the unit.* On the wrong side of an untrimmed half-square-triangle unit, draw a diagonal line perpendicular to the seam line.

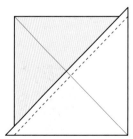

Untrimmed half-square-triangle unit

2. With right sides together and the dark and light triangles opposite each other, place the marked unit on top of a second half-square-triangle unit. Stitch a "slim" ¼" seam on both sides of the diagonal line (see box on page 13).

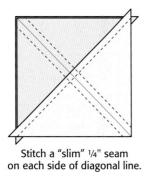

Stitch a "slim" ¼" seam
on each side of diagonal line.

3. Cut on the diagonal line.

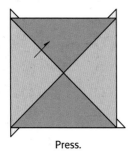

4. Set the stitching and press the seam allowance to one side in each of the 2 resulting units.

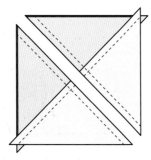

Press.

5. Align the 45° diagonal line of the ruler along one of the seam lines. Position the ruler so that the fabric extends past the ruler on 2 adjacent sides and the remaining 2 sides extend past the 4" lines

of the ruler, *with the 4" lines meeting the seam lines.* Trim away the fabric that extends past the ruler.

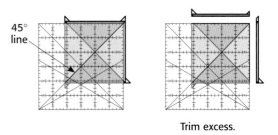

Trim excess.

6. Reposition the unit so that the 2 trimmed edges line up with the 4" lines on the ruler and the diagonal ruler line is aligned with the diagonal seam line. Trim away the remaining 2 edges.

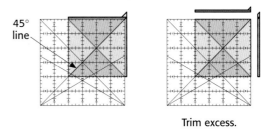

Trim excess.

You should have a perfect, 4"-square hourglass unit.

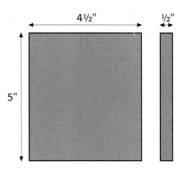

Hourglass unit

*Picket-Fence Units*
1. Trim away ½" from one edge of a 5" square.

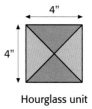

Trim ½" from one edge.

2. In the opposite direction, cut the trimmed piece in half so that the resulting pieces each measure 2½" x 4½".

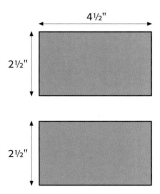

3. Draw a diagonal line on the wrong side of a 2½" square of background fabric. With right sides together, place this 2½" square on top of a 2½" x 4½" rectangle. Stitch one thread width to the outside of the diagonal line. Chain-sew (page 13) several of these at a time.

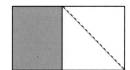

Stitch one thread to the outside of the diagonal line.

**Note:** If you want to make use of the waste triangles, sew ½" to the outside of the first seam; there is no need to mark this seam line. You will trim these small half-square triangles to an exact size when you use them in a future project.

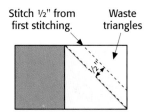

Stitch ½" from first stitching.    Waste triangles

Lightly press to set the seam and cut between the 2 lines of stitching. Set the waste triangle pair aside; then set the seam again in the remaining

unit and press toward the small triangle, unless otherwise directed in the individual block illustrations for the quilt you are making.

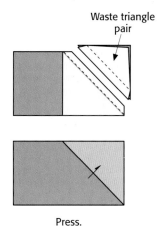

Waste triangle pair

Press.
Picket-fence unit A

4. For a mirror-image pair of picket-fence units, repeat steps 1–3 at the left end of a rectangle.

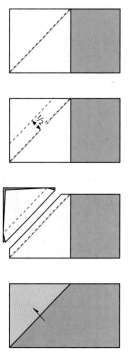

Picket-fence unit B

5. Sew the picket-fence units together in one of the 2 configurations shown, as directed in the instructions for the specific quilt you are making.

Picket-fence unit I     Picket-fence unit II

## Flying-Geese Units

1. Choose 5" squares for the large triangles in the flying-geese units and trim ½" from one edge.

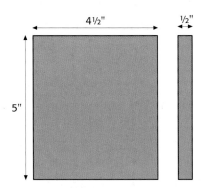

Trim ½" from one edge.

2. In the opposite direction, cut each resulting rectangle in half to yield 2 rectangles, each 2½" x 4½".

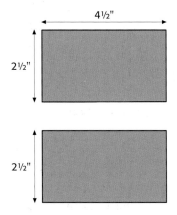

3. Draw a diagonal line on the wrong side of a 2½" square of background fabric. With right sides together, place the marked square on top of a rectangle at the right-hand end. Stitch one thread to the outside of the diagonal line. Chain-sew (page 13) several of these at a time. If you want to save the waste triangles for other projects, refer to the note and illustrations with the directions for the picket-fence units on page 13.

Stitch one thread to the outside
of the diagonal line.

4. Press to set the seam; then press the seam in the flying-geese unit toward the small triangle.

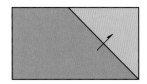

5. Repeat steps 3 and 4 to add a square to the left end of the unit.

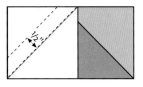

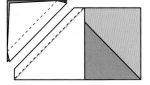

Each flying-geese unit should measure 2½" x 4½".

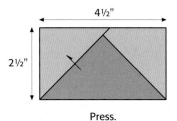

Press.

Flying-geese unit

# ❧ *Finishing Your Quilt* ❧

## Assembling the Quilt Top

You've finished the blocks for your quilt and you're ready to sew them together in a straight or on-point (diagonal) setting. For straight sets, join the blocks in horizontal rows, pressing seams in opposite directions from row to row. Sew the completed rows together.

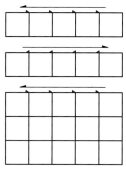

Straight-set quilt

To set blocks on point, you will arrange and sew the blocks and setting triangles together in diagonal rows before joining the rows and adding corner triangles to complete the quilt top. Using a design wall to arrange the blocks for either type of setting arrangement is very helpful, but most especially for on-point settings.

Unless the setting includes sashing strips between the blocks, press the seams in opposite directions from row to row. This helps the seam intersections nestle together for perfectly matched seams in the finished quilt top. When sashing strips and squares are used in a quilt setting, press all seams toward the sashing pieces.

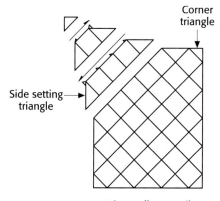

Diagonally set quilt

## Adding the Borders

For the quilts in this book, you will add either straight-cut borders or pieced borders combined with straight-cut inner and outer borders to complete your quilt top.

### Plain Borders

1. To determine the cut length of the side-border strips, measure the quilt-top length through the center. Cut 2 border strips to this length.

2. Fold each strip in half and then in half again and mark the quarter-points at the folds with pins. Fold and pin-mark the quilt-top edges in the same manner.

3. With right sides together and marking pins matching, pin the border strips to the quilt top. Stitch ¼" from the raw edges to attach each border.

4. Press to set the stitching; then press the seam toward the border.

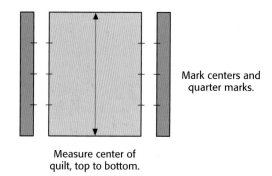

Mark centers and quarter marks.

Measure center of quilt, top to bottom.

5. Measure the quilt width through the center, including the borders you just added. Cut the top- and bottom-border strips to match this measurement. Pin-mark the borders and the quilt top as you did for the side borders. Pin, stitch, and press.

If your quilt has multiple plain borders, repeat steps 1–5 to attach each additional border.

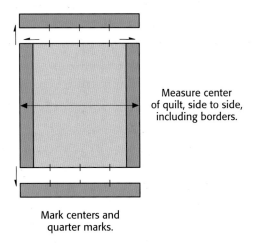

Measure center of quilt, side to side, including borders.

Mark centers and quarter marks.

## Pieced Borders

Whenever a quilt in this book has pieced borders, it also has an inner or "spacer" border and an outer plain border.

**Note:** The cut width for the inner borders as given in the cutting table for each quilt is correct, *but only if all of your piecing seams were 100 percent accurate throughout the block and quilt-top assembly. It is best to wait to cut the inner borders until the blocks have been joined to create the quilt top.*

1. Measure the quilt-top length and width through the center and subtract ½" from each dimension for seam allowances.

2. Measure the length of the top and bottom pieced borders. Subtract the finished size of the 2 corner units plus ½" inch for seam allowances from each pieced-border measurement.

3. Compare the measurements of the top and bottom pieced-border strips. *If they are not the same, you must adjust them so they are before you go any further.* Repeat with the side-border strips. To adjust them, take in or let out seam allowances to make them equal.

4. Use the formula as shown in the following examples to determine the cut width for the inner-border strips.

| | |
|---|---|
| Length of top & bottom pieced borders | 80" (a) |
| Subtract width of quilt top (step 1 above) | - 75" (b) = 5" (c) |
| Divide (c) by 2 | = 2.5"(d) |
| Add ½" for seam allowances | + .5" = 3" cut width for side inner-border strips |
| Length of side pieced borders | 90" (a) |
| Subtract length of quilt top | - 87" (b) = 3" (c) |
| Divide (c) by 2 | = 1.5" |
| Add ½" for seam allowances | + .5"= 2" width for top and bottom inner borders |

**Note:** In case you're wondering if we've made a mistake—it is true that in some cases, the top and bottom inner-border strips will *not* be the same width as the side inner-border strips.

After you have determined the strip width for the inner borders, add all borders, referring to the direction for "Plain Borders" on page 21.

## Marking the Quilt Top for Quilting

If you have a specific quilting design in mind, mark the quilt top *before* you baste the layers together. (We machine quilt our tops and generally use a random quilting design that doesn't need to be marked.) Be sure to test the marking tool you've chosen on a scrap of fabric to be sure you can remove it later.

## Making the Quilt Backing

It is usually necessary to piece the backing for a quilt. To make sure you use the backing yardage correctly (so you don't run short), choose the illustration on the facing page that most closely matches the quilt-top dimensions. Cut the yardage into the required number of pieces.

Since selvages shrink at a different rate than the remainder of the quilt and cause the backing seams to pucker, *it is important to remove all selvages from the backing fabric before piecing the backing.*

The measurements shown below allow for an additional 2" of backing on each side of the quilt. If you are going to have your quilt professionally quilted, you will want to add at least another 2" on each side.

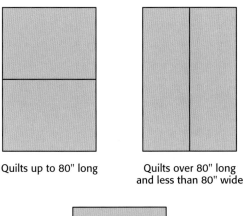

Quilts up to 80" long

Quilts over 80" long and less than 80" wide

Quilts over 80" wide

## Layering, Basting, and Quilting

You are ready to make a "quilt sandwich."

1. Place the backing face down on a large, smooth, flat surface—a large table or 2 pushed together, or on the floor if you must. Smooth out any wrinkles and use masking tape to secure the backing to the surface. Make sure it is on grain and taut.

### ✦ Nickel Tip ✦

If you are layering your quilt on a carpeted floor, use large "T" pins to pin the backing to the carpet and pad.

2. Arrange the batting on top of the backing and smooth into place.

### ✦ Nickel Tip ✦

If you have purchased a packaged batting, it's a good idea to remove it and lay it out over a bed or across the back of a couch overnight to let it breathe and relax a bit.

3. Place the quilt top, face up, on top of the batting.

4. Pin or hand baste the layers together. For pin basting, place pins approximately every 4"to 6". If you are thread basting, begin in the center of the quilt and work out in opposite directions, first toward the top, and then toward the bottom, through the center of the quilt. Use large stitches for this—at least 2" in length. Next, start in the center again and work to the right and left. Continue in this manner until the entire top is basted in a grid, with stitched lines spaced approximately 4" to 5" apart. It's a good idea to baste diagonally across the quilt in both directions, too.

5. Hand or machine quilt as desired.

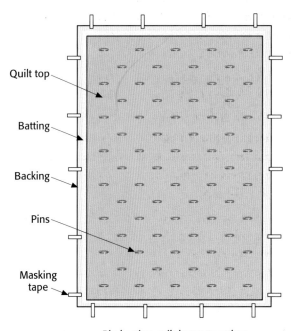

Quilt top

Batting

Backing

Pins

Masking tape

Pin basting quilt layers together

6. Trim the excess batting and backing even with the quilt-top edges, making sure all of the corners are square.

# Adding the Binding

Good work! You're almost done. It's time to add the binding. We used a straight-grain, French (double-layer) binding for all of the quilts in this book.

1. Sew the binding strips together to create one long piece. Use bias seams as shown and press all seams open.

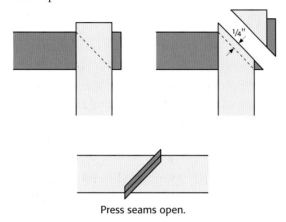

Press seams open.

2. Fold the binding strip in half lengthwise with wrong sides together and raw edges even.

3. If available, attach a walking foot or engage the even-feed feature on your machine. Beginning in the center at the bottom edge of the quilt and leaving the first 10" of the binding free from the stitching, stitch ¼" from the raw edges. Stitch to the corner of the quilt, stopping ¼" from the raw edge, and backstitch 1 or 2 stitches. Clip the threads.

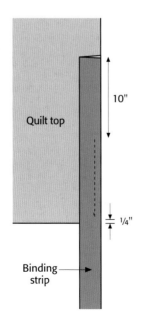

Quilt top

10"

¼"

Binding strip

4. Remove the quilt from the machine and rotate it ¼ turn to the left. Fold the binding strip up and away from the quilt, forming a 45°-angle fold at the corner. Holding the fold in place with a pin, fold the binding back onto the quilt to form a fold parallel to and even with the quilt-top raw edge.

5. With the raw edges of the binding even with the quilt edges, stitch from the fold, ending and back-stitching ¼" from the next corner. Continue around the remaining sides of the quilt in the same manner, stopping approximately 12" from where you started stitching.

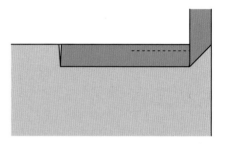

Now, you're ready to join the binding ends. We prefer to sew the binding ends together at an angle so you can't really tell where the binding begins or ends.

6. Position the raw edges of the beginning end of the binding even with the quilt raw edges. Position the remaining end on top. On the lower strip, trim away the excess, leaving a 2½" allowance (the width of the unpressed binding strip).

7. Open out both ends of the binding and align as shown. Pin the ends together and draw a 45°-angle line from corner to corner.

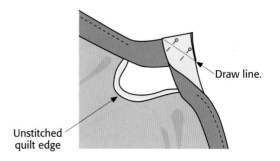

Draw line.

Unstitched quilt edge

8. Stitch on the line. Press the seam open; then trim to ¼". (If you press *before* you trim, you'll have a little more fabric to handle and lessen the likelihood of burning your fingers on the iron!)

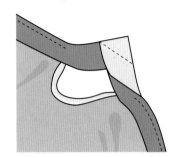

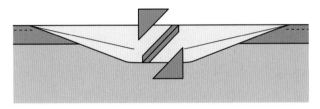

Press open and trim to ¼".

9. Refold the binding and stitch to the quilt top, overlapping the beginning and ending stitches.

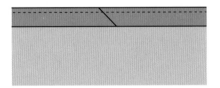

## Labeling Your Quilt

Congratulations! Now you have a finished quilt—well, almost. The very last step is adding a label to document your work. Even though you may not think of your quilt as a work of art, years later when it's been passed down a generation or two (and shows up on an antique appraisal show on TV), the future owner will appreciate any available information.

Your label doesn't have to be fancy—but it can be as elaborate as you wish to make it. For the simplest label, use a permanent fabric marking pen to write pertinent information on a piece of plain muslin. Include your name, the name of the quilt pattern, the date you started your project, and perhaps the date you finished. (Sometimes that date can be a bit embarrassing, but include it anyway; it can spark some interesting stories.) If the quilt is a gift, include the name of the recipient and the occasion for which it was made.

Some quilters like to keep a short documentation sheet, along with a photo of the quilt, in a personal quilt album. Include the same information you put on the label along with other pertinent information, such as notes about the fabric and any changes you may have made to the design. Perhaps you will want to include information about the fabric trade that provided the nickel squares for the quilt.

# *The Quilt Patterns*

# ❋ Jewel Box ❋

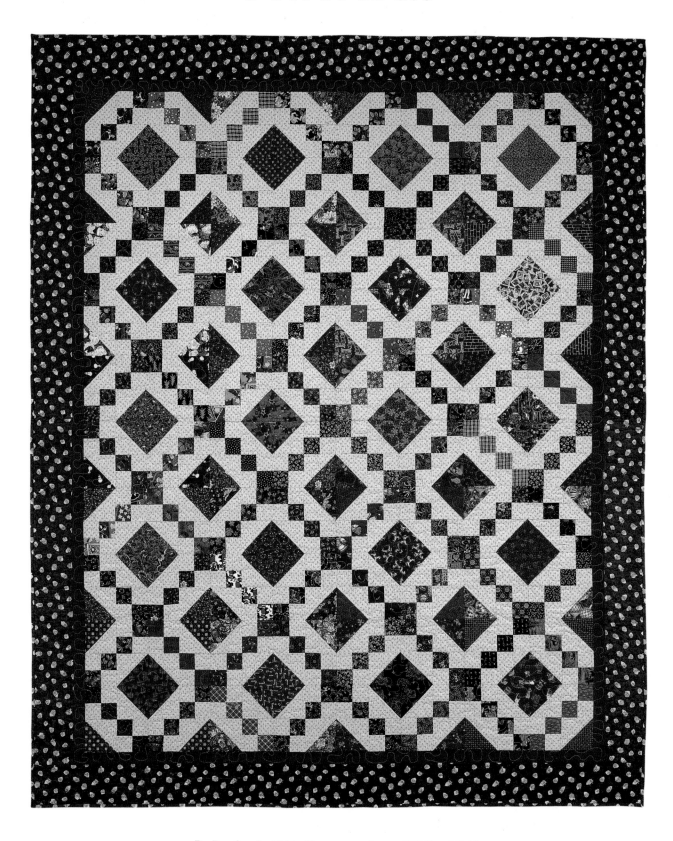

*By Pat Speth, 1997, Davenport, Iowa, 77½" x 93½".*
*Finished block size: 16"*

*T*he size of the easy-to-piece Jewel Box block makes it easy to finish your quilt top in record time. Pat used a variety of red Christmas prints for the block centers and corners and an assortment of green, blue, and black Christmas prints for the four-patch units. These colors simply glow on the yellow gold–print background. Choose a different background color, and the quilt changes dramatically. Try white for more sparkle or tan or light brown for a warmer, cozier look.

Although there are two pairs of reds in each block—one pair for the corner triangle units and one for the center units—scrappy corners and centers are just as effective in this traditional design.

➦ *Skill level:* Beginner

## Quilt Sizes and Statistics

|  | Lap | Twin | Queen |
|---|---|---|---|
| Size | 61½" x 77½" | 77½" x 93½" | 93½" x 109½" |
| Number of blocks | 12 | 20 | 30 |
| Block set | 3 x 4 | 4 x 5 | 5 x 6 |

## Materials

*42"-wide fabric (40" of usable width after preshrinking and removing selvages)*

|  | Lap | Twin | Queen |
|---|---|---|---|
| 5" red squares | 24 pairs | 40 pairs | 60 pairs |
| 5" green, blue, and black squares | 48 | 80 | 120 |
| Background | 1⅞ yds. | 3 yds. | 4⅜ yds. |
| Inner border | ½ yd. | ⅝ yd. | ⅔ yd. |
| Outer border and binding | 1⅞ yds. | 2⅛ yds. | 2½ yds. |
| Backing | 3⅞ yds. | 5⅔ yds. | 8⅜ yds. |
| Batting | 66" x 82" | 82" x 98" | 102" x 118" |

## Cutting

*Cut all strips across the fabric width (crosswise grain).*

### *Lap Size*

|  | First Cut | | Second Cut | |
|---|---|---|---|---|
|  | Number of Strips | Strip Width | Number of Pieces | Piece Size |
| Background | 12 | 5" | 96 | 5" x 5" |
| Inner border | 7 | 2" | | |
| Outer border | 7 | 5½" | | |
| Binding | 8 | 2½" | | |

### *Twin Size*

|  | First Cut | | Second Cut | |
|---|---|---|---|---|
|  | Number of Strips | Strip Width | Number of Pieces | Piece Size |
| Background | 20 | 5" | 160 | 5" x 5" |
| Inner border | 8 | 2" | | |
| Outer border | 8 | 5½" | | |
| Binding | 9 | 2½" | | |

### *Queen Size*

|  | First Cut | | Second Cut | |
|---|---|---|---|---|
|  | Number of Strips | Strip Width | Number of Pieces | Piece Size |
| Background | 30 | 5" | 240 | 5" x 5" |
| Inner border | 9 | 2" | | |
| Outer border | 10 | 5½" | | |
| Binding | 11 | 2½" | | |

## Making the Blocks

For each block you will need:
    2 pairs of red 5" squares
    4 assorted green, blue, and black 5" squares
    8 background 5" squares

1. Referring to "Four-Patch Units" and "Half-Square-Triangle Units" on page 14, make 8 of each unit.

Make 8
for each block.
        Make 8
for each block.

2. Arrange and sew the units from step 1 into the rows shown. Sew the rows together to complete each block. Make the required number of blocks for the quilt size you are making.

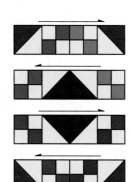

Jewel Box block

## Assembling the Quilt Top

1. Following the quilt plan, arrange the blocks in rows on your design wall.

2. Sew the blocks together in horizontal rows and press the seams in opposite directions from row to row.

3. Referring to "Plain Borders" on page 21, add the inner and outer borders.

## Finishing

1. Layer the quilt top with batting and backing; hand or machine baste the layers together (see page 23).

2. Quilt as desired, bind the edges, add a label, and enjoy your finished quilt.

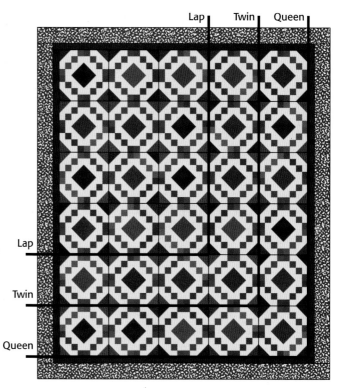

Quilt Plan

# *Autumn Stretched Star*

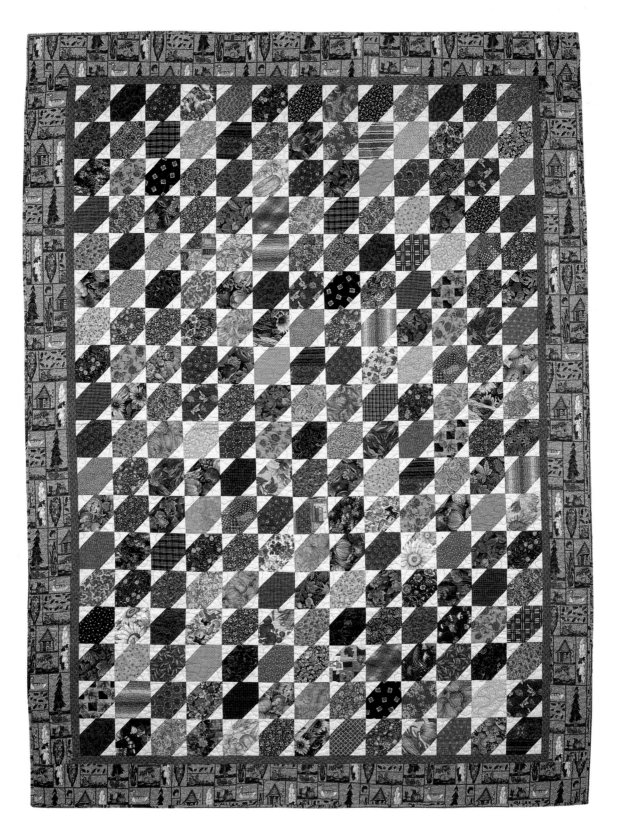

*By Pat Speth, 1997, Davenport, Iowa, 71" x 93½".*
*Finished block size: 4½"*

*T*his colorful quilt was created with the squares from a fall-theme fabric trade. It would also make a great quilt for a child when made from novelty prints with juvenile themes.

→ *Skill level:* Beginner

## Quilt Sizes and Statistics

|  | Lap | Twin | Queen |
|---|---|---|---|
| Size | 62" x 62" | 71" x 93½" | 107" x 107" |
| Number of blocks | 121 | 234 | 441 |
| Block set | 11 x 11 | 13 x 18 | 21 x 21 |

## Materials

*42"-wide fabric (40" of usable width after preshrinking and removing selvages)*

|  | Lap | Twin | Queen |
|---|---|---|---|
| Background | 1⅜ yds. | 2⅓ yds. | 4⅛ yds. |
| 5" squares | 121 | 234 | 441 |
| Inner border | ⅜ yd. | ½ yd. | ⅝ yd. |
| Outer border and binding | 1¾ yds. | 2 yds. | 2¾ yds. |
| Backing | 3⅞ yds. | 5⅔ yds. | 9⅝ yds. |
| Batting | 66" x 66" | 75" x 98" | 111" x 111" |

## Cutting

*Cut all strips across the fabric width (crosswise grain).*

*Lap Size*

|  | First Cut | | Second Cut | |
|---|---|---|---|---|
|  | Number of Strips | Strip Width | Number of Pieces | Piece Size |
| Background | 16 | 2½" | 242 | 2½" x 2½" |
| Inner border | 6 | 1½" | | |
| Outer border | 7 | 5½" | | |
| Binding | 7 | 2½" | | |

*Twin Size*

|  | First Cut | | Second Cut | |
|---|---|---|---|---|
|  | Number of Strips | Strip Width | Number of Pieces | Piece Size |
| Background | 30 | 2½" | 468 | 2½" x 2½" |
| Inner border | 7 | 1½" | | |
| Outer border | 8 | 5½" | | |
| Binding | 9 | 2½" | | |

*Queen Size*

|  | First Cut | | Second Cut | |
|---|---|---|---|---|
|  | Number of Strips | Strip Width | Number of Pieces | Piece Size |
| Background | 56 | 2½" | 882 | 2½" x 2½" |
| Inner border | 10 | 1½" | | |
| Outer border | 11 | 5½" | | |
| Binding | 12 | 2½" | | |

## Making the Blocks

1. For each block, draw a diagonal line on the wrong side of two 2½" squares of background fabric (for the star points). With right sides together, place a marked square at one corner of a 5" square. Stitch, referring to "Sew and Flip" on page 15 and "Waste Triangles" on page 15. Chain-sew several blocks at a time.

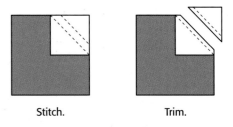

Stitch.          Trim.

2. Press the seam toward the triangle.

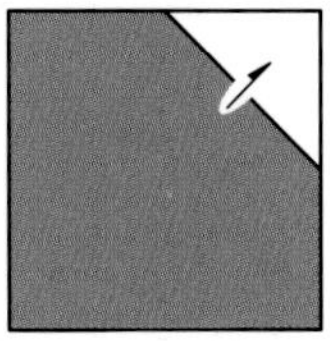

Press.

3. Repeat steps 1 and 2 to add a triangle to the lower left corner and complete the block. Make the required number of blocks for the quilt size you are making.

Stretched Star block

## Assembling the Quilt Top

1. Following the quilt plan for the size you are making, arrange the blocks on a design wall as desired. You may also use one of the alternate block arrangements shown.

  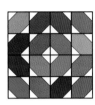

Alternate block arrangements

2. Sew the finished blocks together in horizontal rows and press the seams in opposite directions from row to row.

3. Referring to "Plain Borders" on page 21, add the inner and outer borders.

## Finishing

1. Layer the quilt top with batting and backing; hand or machine baste the layers together (see page 23).

2. Quilt as desired, bind the edges, add a label, and enjoy your finished quilt.

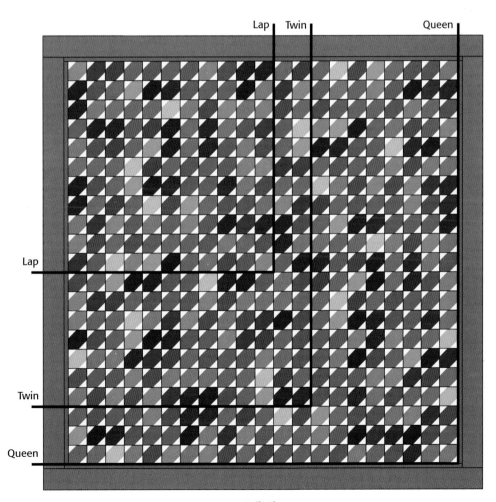

Quilt Plan

# Sunny Lanes

*By Pat Speth, 1998, Davenport, Iowa, 92½" x 108½".*
*Finished block size: 16"*

*A*lthough it looks complex, this quilt is a breeze to make with half-square-triangle and four-patch units. It's a great way to use up any assortment of 5" squares. These came from a trade that took place at a quilting retreat. There's a little bit of everything in the fabric selection—even Elvis makes a cameo appearance in this quilt!

❧ *Skill level:* Beginner

## Quilt Sizes and Statistics

|  | Twin | Full | Queen |
|---|---|---|---|
| Size | 76½" x 92½" | 92½" x 108½" | 108½" x 108½" |
| Number of blocks | 20 | 30 | 36 |
| Block set | 4 x 5 | 5 x 6 | 6 x 6 |

## Materials

*42"-wide fabric (40" of usable width after preshrinking and removing selvages)*

|  | Twin | Full | Queen |
|---|---|---|---|
| 5" dark squares | 160 | 240 | 288 |
| Background | 3 yds. | 4⅜ yds. | 5¼ yds. |
| Inner border | ½ yd. | ½ yd. | ⅝ yd. |
| Outer border and binding | 2⅛ yds. | 2½ yds. | 2¾ yds. |
| Backing | 5⅝ yds. | 8¼ yds. | 9⅝ yds. |
| Batting | 81" x 81" | 97" x 113" | 113" x 113" |

## Cutting

*Cut all strips across the fabric width (crosswise grain).*

### *Twin Size*

|  | First Cut | | Second Cut | |
|---|---|---|---|---|
|  | Number of Strips | Strip Width | Number of Pieces | Piece Size |
| Background | 20 | 5" | 160 | 5" x 5" |
| Inner border | 8 | 1½" | | |
| Outer border | 8 | 5½" | | |
| Binding | 9 | 2½" | | |

### *Full Size*

|  | First Cut | | Second Cut | |
|---|---|---|---|---|
|  | Number of Strips | Strip Width | Number of Pieces | Piece Size |
| Background | 30 | 5" | 240 | 5" x 5" |
| Inner border | 9 | 1½" | | |
| Outer border | 10 | 5½" | | |
| Binding | 11 | 2½" | | |

### *Queen Size*

|  | First Cut | | Second Cut | |
|---|---|---|---|---|
|  | Number of Strips | Strip Width | Number of Pieces | Piece Size |
| Background | 36 | 5" | 288 | 5" x 5" |
| Inner border | 10 | 1½" | | |
| Outer border | 11 | 5½" | | |
| Binding | 12 | 2½" | | |

## Making the Blocks

For each block you will need:

    8 dark 5" squares
    8 background 5" squares

1. Referring to "Four-Patch Units" on page 14, sew dark squares and background squares together to yield 8 four-patch units. Make 8 four-patch units for each block.

Make 8
for each block.

2. Referring to "Half-Square-Triangle Units" on page 14, sew 4 background squares and 4 dark squares together to yield 8 half-square-triangle units for each block.

Make 8
for each block.

3. For each block, arrange the units from steps 1 and 2 into the 4 rows shown, taking care to orient the half-square-triangle units correctly in each row. Sew the units together in rows and press in the direction of the arrows.

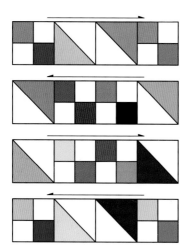

4. Sew the rows together to complete each block and press in the direction of the arrow. Make the required number of Sunny Lanes blocks for the quilt size you are making.

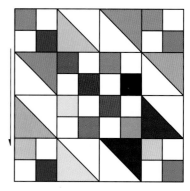

Sunny Lanes block

## Assembling the Quilt Top

1. Arrange the blocks on a design wall, turning every other block one-quarter turn to form the design. Check the layout against the plan to make sure the blocks are correctly arranged.

Block rotated 1/4 turn

2. Sew the blocks together in horizontal rows and press the seams in opposite directions from row to row.

3. Referring to "Plain Borders" on page 21, add the inner and outer borders.

## Finishing

1. Layer the quilt top with batting and backing; hand or machine baste the layers together (see page 23).

2. Quilt as desired, bind the edges, add a label, and enjoy your finished quilt.

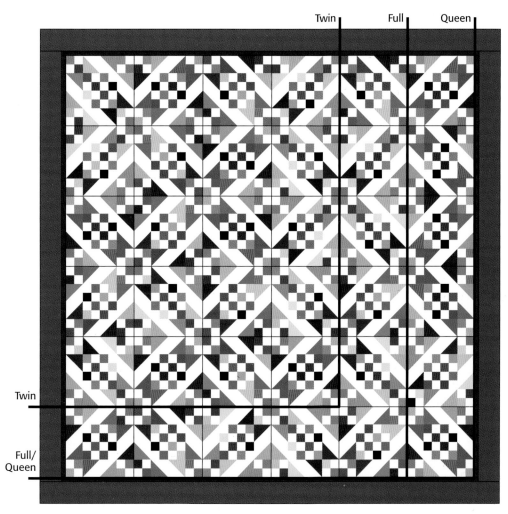

Twin    Full    Queen

Twin

Full/
Queen

Quilt Plan

# ☀ *Northern Lights* ☀

By Pat Speth, 1997, Davenport, Iowa, 77½" x 101½".
Finished block size: 8"

*N orthern Lights"* features a collection of Christmas fabrics in an assortment of color families on a warm, gold background. The blocks were arranged by color in a barn-raising set so that the rows radiate from the center.

→ *Skill level:* Beginner

## Quilt Sizes and Statistics

|  | Lap | Full | Queen |
|---|---|---|---|
| Size | 61½" x 77½" | 77½" x 101½" | 93½" x 101½" |
| Number of blocks | 48 | 88 | 110 |
| Block set | 6 x 8 | 8 x 11 | 10 x 11 |

## Materials

*42"-wide fabric (40" of usable width after preshrinking and removing selvages)*

|  | Lap | Full | Queen |
|---|---|---|---|
| Assorted 5" squares in Christmas prints | 48 pairs | 88 pairs | 110 pairs |
| Background | 1⅞ yds. | 3⅜ yds. | 4¼ yds. |
| Inner border | ½ yd. | ⅝ yd. | ¾ yd. |
| Outer border and binding | 1⅞ yds. | 2⅜ yds. | 2½ yds. |
| Backing | 3⅞ yds. | 6⅛ yds. | 8⅜ yds. |
| Batting | 66" x 82" | 82" x 106" | 98" x 106" |

## Cutting

*Cut all strips across the fabric width (crosswise grain).*

### Lap Size

|  | First Cut | | Second Cut | |
|---|---|---|---|---|
|  | Number of Strips | Strip Width | Number of Pieces | Piece Size |
| Background | 12 | 5" | 96 | 5" x 5" |
| Inner border | 7 | 2" | | |
| Outer border | 7 | 5½" | | |
| Binding | 8 | 2½" | | |

### Full Size

|  | First Cut | | Second Cut | |
|---|---|---|---|---|
|  | Number of Strips | Strip Width | Number of Pieces | Piece Size |
| Background | 22 | 5" | 176 | 5" x 5" |
| Inner border | 9 | 2" | | |
| Outer border | 9 | 5½" | | |
| Binding | 10 | 2½" | | |

### Queen Size

|  | First Cut | | Second Cut | |
|---|---|---|---|---|
|  | Number of Strips | Strip Width | Number of Pieces | Piece Size |
| Background | 28 | 5" | 220 | 5" x 5" |
| Inner border | 10 | 2" | | |
| Outer border | 10 | 5½" | | |
| Binding | 11 | 2½" | | |

## Making the Blocks

For each block you will need:

    1 pair of 5" Christmas squares

    1 pair of 5" background squares

1. Referring to "Half-Square-Triangle Units" and "Four-Patch Units" on page 14, and using the fabric pairs, make 2 four-patch units and 2 half-square-triangle units.

    Make 2             Make 2
 for each block.     for each block.

2. Arrange the units from step 1 in 2 horizontal rows. Sew together in rows and press the seams toward the half-square-triangle unit in each row.

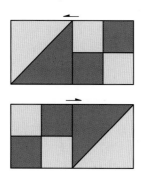

3. Join the rows to complete the block. Press. Make the required number of blocks for the quilt size you are making.

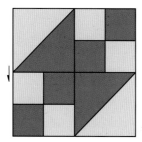

Northern Lights block

## Assembling the Quilt Top

1. Referring to the quilt plan, arrange the blocks in a barn-raising set on your design wall.

2. Sew the blocks together in horizontal rows and press the seams in opposite directions from row to row.

3. Referring to "Plain Borders" on page 21, measure the quilt top to determine the cut length of the side inner and outer borders. Sew the inner-border strips to the outer-border strips and press the seams toward the outer border. Sew the combined side borders to the quilt top and press the seam toward the borders.

4. Repeat step 3 to add combined top and bottom borders to the quilt top.

## Finishing

1. Layer the quilt top with batting and backing; hand or machine baste the layers together (see page 23).

2. Quilt as desired, bind the edges, add a label, and enjoy your finished quilt.

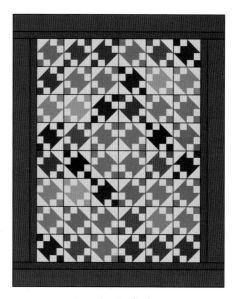

Lap-Size Quilt Plan

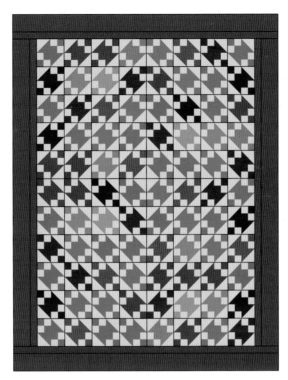

Full-Size Quilt Plan

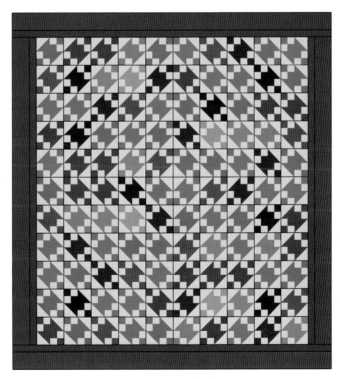

Queen-Size Quilt Plan

# ❊ Four-Patch Plaid ❊

*By Pat Speth, 2000, Davenport, Iowa, 68½" x 96½".*

*T*rust us! This wonderful quilt is much easier than it might appear at first glance! You'll make an assortment of two-patch, four-patch, and picket-fence units to create it. For a warm look, Pat used plaids and prints in dark and medium tones. A variety of creams, tans, and golds add to the feeling. Combine plaids and prints in the two-patch and four-patch units to duplicate the effect that Pat achieved. As this is a strip quilt, we do not list a finished block size.

✦ *Skill level:* Easy

## Quilt Sizes and Statistics

|  | Lap | Twin | Queen |
|---|---|---|---|
| Size | 68½" x 68½" | 68½" x 96½" | 104½" x 104½" |
| Block set | 13 x 13 | 13 x 20 | 22 x 22 |
| Two-patch units | 46 | 73 | 133 |
| Four-patch units | 89 | 134 | 246 |
| Picket-fence unit A (print) | 56 | 70 | 92 |
| Picket-fence unit B (plaid) | 56 | 70 | 92 |
| Background squares | 38 | 57 | 109 |

## Materials

*42"-wide fabric (40" of usable width after preshrinking and removing selvages)*

|  | Lap | Twin | Queen |
|---|---|---|---|
| 5" plaid squares | 74 | 105 | 174 |
| 5" print squares | 74 | 105 | 174 |
| 5" cream squares | 73 | 102 | 169 |
| 4½" cream squares* | 38 | 57 | 109 |
| Borders and binding | 1¾ yds. | 1⅞ yds. | 2⅜ yds. |
| Backing | 4¼ yds. | 5⅞ yds. | 9⅜ yds. |
| Batting | 73" x 73" | 73" x 101" | 109" x 109" |

*\* If you already have an assortment of 5" cream squares, simply trim the squares to 4½" x 4½".*

## Cutting

*Cut all strips across the fabric width (crosswise grain).*
**Note:** Wait to cut the strips for the inner border until the quilt top is finished (see "Pieced Borders" on page 22).

### *Lap Size*

|  | Number of Strips | Strip Width |
|---|---|---|
| Inner border | 6 | 2½" |
| Outer border | 8 | 2½" |
| Binding | 8 | 2½" |

### *Twin Size*

|  | Number of Strips | Strip Width |
|---|---|---|
| Inner border | 7 | 2½" |
| Outer border | 8 | 2½" |
| Binding | 9 | 2½" |

### *Queen Size*

|  | Number of Strips | Strip Width |
|---|---|---|
| Inner border | 10 | 2½" |
| Outer border | 10 | 2½" |
| Binding | 11 | 2½" |

## Making the Units

Referring to "Two-Patch Units" and "Four-Patch Units" on page 14, make the required number of two-patch and four-patch units. Combine plaids and prints in each of the units.

## Assembling the Quilt Top

1. Referring to the quilt plan, arrange the two-patch units, four-patch units, and 4½" squares on your design wall in the 6 horizontal rows shown. Make the required number of each row for the quilt size you are making. Sew the units together in each row and press in the direction of the arrows—always toward the two-patch units or the cream squares.

**Note:** The illustrations show the correct number of units in each horizontal row for the lap and twin sizes. Refer to the quilt plan to extend the rows for the queen size.

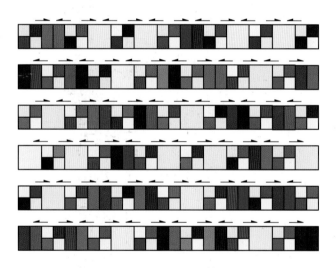

2. Sew the rows together to create the quilt top.

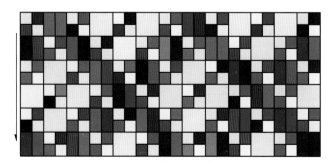

## ✦ Nickel Tip ✦

Join the completed horizontal rows in groups of 3 to 5, and then sew the sections together. Number the rows on the quilt diagram using sticky notes to keep track of where you are.

## Making the Pieced Border

1. Referring to "Picket-Fence Units" on page 18, make the required number of units for the borders (see "Quilt Sizes and Statistics" on page 43). Using 1 plaid and 1 print fabric for each unit, position them as shown in the illustration. Press the seams toward the print and away from the plaid so the seams will nestle together for a perfectly matched point when you sew units A and B together to create a Picket Fence block.

Picket Fence block

2. Refer to "Pieced Borders" on page 22 to cut and add the inner, pieced, and outer borders.

## Finishing

1. Layer the quilt top with batting and backing; hand or machine baste the layers together (see page 23).

2. Quilt as desired, bind the edges, add a label, and enjoy your finished quilt.

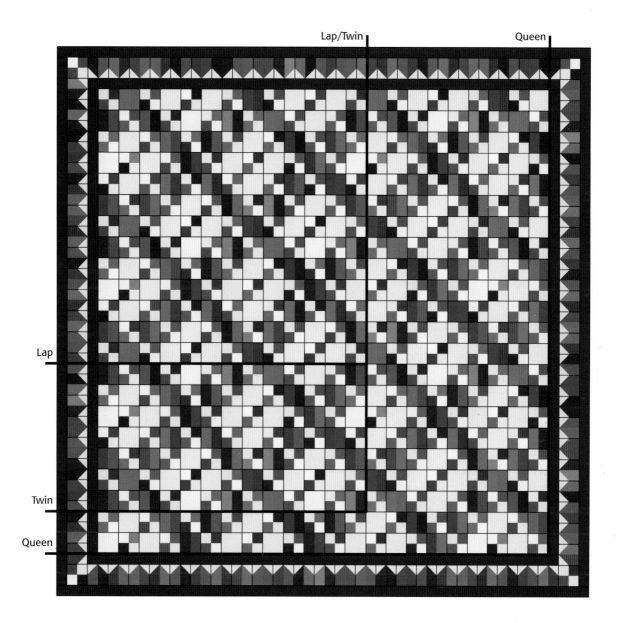

Lap/Twin  Queen

Lap

Twin

Queen

# ❋ Millennium Star ❋

*By Robin Korth, 2000, Davenport, Iowa, 72½" x 96½".*
*Finished block size: 12"*

*I*f you have some of the millennium-style fabrics marketed to commemorate the year 2000, here's the perfect place to use them—or another favorite theme fabric. Since this quilt features a single background fabric, some of the block construction is accomplished with strip piecing.

➤ *Skill level:* Easy

## Quilt Sizes and Statistics

|  | Lap | Twin | Queen |
|---|---|---|---|
| Size | 60½" x 60½" | 72½" x 96½" | 108½" x 108½" |
| Number of blocks | 16 | 35 | 64 |
| Block set | 4 x 4 | 5 x 7 | 8 x 8 |

## Materials

*42"-wide fabric (40" of usable width after preshrinking and removing selvages)*

|  | Lap | Twin | Queen |
|---|---|---|---|
| Dark blue* | 1⅔ yds. | 3 yds. | 4⅛ yds. |
| Background | 1⅝ yds. | 3⅜ yds. | 5¾ yds. |
| Assorted 5" squares | 32 pairs | 70 pairs | 128 pairs |
| Inner border and binding | ⅞ yd. | 1⅛ yds. | 1½ yds. |
| Backing | 3⅞ yds. | 5⅞ yds. | 9⅝ yds. |
| Batting | 65" x 65" | 77" x 101" | 113" x 113" |

* Millennium fabric

## Cutting

### Lap Size

|  | First Cut | | Second Cut | |
|---|---|---|---|---|
|  | Number of Strips | Strip Width | Number of Pieces | Piece Size |
| Dark blue* | 2 | 4½" | 16 | 4½" x 4½" |
| Dark blue* | 4 | 2½" | | |

*continued*

### Lap Size continued

|  | First Cut | | Second Cut | |
|---|---|---|---|---|
|  | Number of Strips | Strip Width | Number of Pieces | Piece Size |
| Background | 8 | 2½" | 128 | 2½" x 2½" |
| Background | 8 | 2½" | 64 | 2½" x 4½" |
| Background | 4 | 2½" | | |
| Inner border | 6 | 1½" | | |
| Outer border* | 6 | 5½" | | |
| Binding | 7 | 2½" | | |

### Twin Size

|  | First Cut | | Second Cut | |
|---|---|---|---|---|
|  | Number of Strips | Strip Width | Number of Pieces | Piece Size |
| Dark blue* | 5 | 4½" | 35 | 4½" x 4½" |
| Dark blue* | 9 | 2½" | | |
| Background | 18 | 2½" | 280 | 2½" x 2½" |
| Background | 18 | 2½" | 140 | 2½" x 4½" |
| Background | 9 | 2½" | | |
| Inner border | 8 | 1½" | | |
| Outer border* | 9 | 5½" | | |
| Binding | 9 | 2½" | | |

### Queen Size

|  | First Cut | | Second Cut | |
|---|---|---|---|---|
|  | Number of Strips | Strip Width | Number of Pieces | Piece Size |
| Dark blue* | 8 | 4½" | 64 | 4½" x 4½" |
| Dark blue* | 16 | 2½" | | |
| Background | 32 | 2½" | 512 | 2½" x 2½" |
| Background | 32 | 2½" | 256 | 2½" x 4½" |
| Background | 16 | 2½" | | |
| Inner border | 10 | 1½" | | |
| Outer border* | 11 | 5½" | | |
| Binding | 12 | 2½" | | |

* Millennium fabric

## Making the Blocks

For each block you will need:

- 4 two-patch units (see steps 1 and 2, below)
- 4 background pieces, each 2½" x 4½"
- 2 pairs of dark 5" squares for the 4 sets of picket-fence units
- 8 background 2½" squares
- 1 dark blue (millennium) 4½" square

1. Sew the 2½"-wide strips of dark blue (millennium) and background fabrics together in pairs, using ¼"-wide seam allowances. Press toward the dark blue strip.

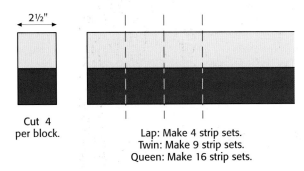

2. Cut the strip sets from step 1 into 2½"-wide units. You will need 4 for each block in your quilt.

Cut 4 per block.

Lap: Make 4 strip sets.
Twin: Make 9 strip sets.
Queen: Make 16 strip sets.

3. Sew each unit from step 2 to a 2½" x 4½" piece of background fabric, making 2 with the pieced unit on the left (corner-unit A) and 2 with the pieced unit on the right (corner-unit B) for each block. Press the seams toward the background rectangle in each resulting corner unit.

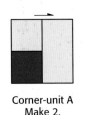

Corner-unit A
Make 2.

Corner-unit B
Make 2.

4. Trim away ½" from one side of each of the 4 dark squares for the picket-fence units. In the opposite direction, cut each piece in half to yield 8 rectangles, each 2½" x 4½".

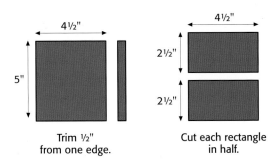

Trim ½" from one edge.

Cut each rectangle in half.

5. Referring to "Picket-Fence Units" on page 18 and "Waste Triangles" on page 15, sew a 2½" square of background fabric to the right end of 4 of the rectangles from step 4. Repeat with the remaining rectangles, adding the background square to the left end. Press seams in the direction of the arrows. *You will press toward the triangle in one set and away in the second set* so the seams will match perfectly when you join the units to make the star points.

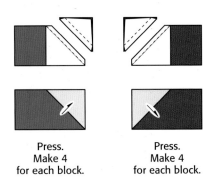

Press.
Make 4
for each block.

Press.
Make 4
for each block.

6. Sew the picket-fence units together in pairs to make 4 star-point units for each block. Press.

Make 4 star points
for each block.

7. Arrange the corner and star-point units with a 4½" square of dark blue fabric to create 3 horizontal rows. Sew the units together in each row and press seams in the direction of the arrows.

8. Sew the rows together and press all seams away from the star-point units to complete each block. Make the required number of blocks for the quilt size you are making.

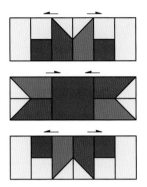

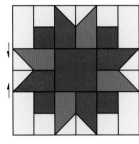

Millennium Star block

## Assembling the Quilt Top

1. Referring to the quilt plan, arrange the blocks on a design wall. For perfectly matched seam intersections, block to block and row to row, rotate the blocks as needed so the seams will nestle together when you stitch them. Sew the blocks together in horizontal rows and press the seams in opposite directions from row to row.

2. Sew the rows together and press.

3. Add the inner and outer borders, referring to "Plain Borders" on page 21.

## Finishing

1. Layer the quilt top with batting and backing; hand or machine baste the layers together (see page 23).

2. Quilt as desired, bind the edges, add a label, and enjoy your finished quilt.

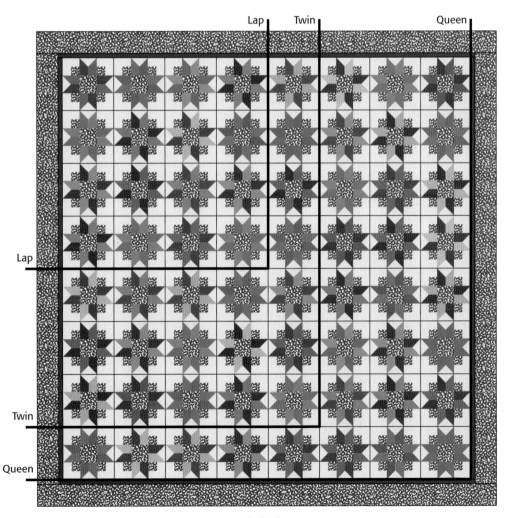

Quilt Plan

# Paducah Nine Patch

*By Pat Speth, 1999, Davenport, Iowa, 64½" x 88½".*
*Finished block size: 8"*

*T*he reproduction prints (1850–1900) in "Paducah Nine Patch" create a wonderful, old-fashioned look. (Be sure to thank your quilt shop owners for carrying these wonderful fabrics!) To save time in cutting and assembling this block, cut and sew at least two blocks at a time.

✦ *Skill level:* Easy

## Quilt Sizes and Statistics

|  | Lap | Twin | Queen |
|---|---|---|---|
| Size | 56½" x 64½" | 64½" x 88½" | 104½" x 104½" |
| Number of blocks | 56 | 88 | 169 |
| Block set | 7 x 8 | 8 x 11 | 13 x 13 |

## Materials

*42"-wide fabric (40" of usable width after preshrinking and removing selvages)*

|  | Lap | Twin | Queen |
|---|---|---|---|
| 5" dark squares | 56 pairs | 88 pairs | 169 pairs |
| 5" medium squares | 56 pairs | 88 pairs | 169 pairs |
| 5" light squares | 56 pairs | 88 pairs | 169 pairs |
| Backing | 3⅝ yds. | 5⅜ yds. | 9⅜ yds. |
| Binding | ⅝ yd. | ¾ yd. | 1 yd. |
| Batting | 61" x 69" | 69" x 93" | 110" x 110" |

## Cutting

*Cut all strips across the fabric width (crosswise grain).*

*Lap Size*

|  | Number of Strips | Strip Width |
|---|---|---|
| Binding | 7 | 2½" |

*Twin Size*

|  | Number of Strips | Strip Width |
|---|---|---|
| Binding | 9 | 2½" |

*Queen Size*

|  | Number of Strips | Strip Width |
|---|---|---|
| Binding | 11 | 2½" |

## Making the Blocks

For each block you will need:
    1 pair of dark 5" squares
    1 pair of medium 5" squares
    1 pair of light 5" squares

**Note:** When assembling the blocks, be sure to alternate the placement of the dark and medium fabrics. Use the dark fabrics in the four-patch units and the center nine-patch units for half of the blocks and the medium fabrics for the large rectangles. Reverse the color placement for the remaining blocks.

1. Position 1 dark (or medium) square and 1 light square with right sides together on your cutting mat. Cut the layered squares into 1½"-wide strips. Without disturbing the layers, sew the strip sets together, as layered, along one long edge of each. Press the seam toward the darker fabric in each unit.

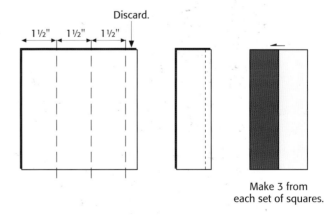

Make 3 from each set of squares.

2. With right sides together and the darker color in one strip against the lighter color in the second strip, place 2 of the units from step 1 on the cutting board. Cut into 1½"-wide segments.

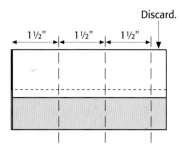

3. Sew the 2 segments together to make a four-patch unit. You will have 1 large two-patch unit left to add to your scrap collection. Press. Make 4 units for each block.

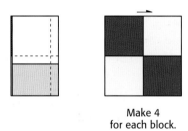

Make 4
for each block.

4. Cut the remaining light 5" square into the pieces shown.

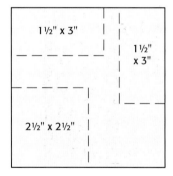

Cut 1 for each block.

## ✦ Nickel Tip ✦

Save time by stacking light squares for more than one block on top of each other and then cutting the stack into the proper sizes. Stack no more than 4 squares together.

5. Cut the remaining dark or medium 5" square into the pieces shown.

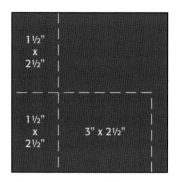

Cut 1 for each block.

6. To make the nine-patch center unit, arrange 2 dark rectangles with a light square and sew together. Press the seams toward the rectangles. Make 1 for each block.

Make 1.

7. Arrange the remaining light and dark pieces and sew together as shown. Press the seams toward the darker fabric. Cut the resulting unit in half horizontally to yield 2 units, each 1½" x 4½".

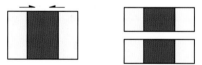

8. Arrange the units from steps 6 and 7 as shown to make the center nine-patch unit. Sew the rows together and press in the direction of the arrows.

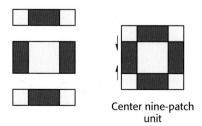

Center nine-patch
unit

9. Trim away ½" from one side of the remaining dark or medium pair of squares. In the opposite direction, cut each resulting large rectangle in half to yield 2 pieces, each 2½" x 4½".

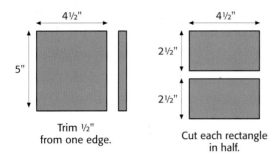

Trim ½"
from one edge.

Cut each rectangle
in half.

10. Arrange the center nine-patch unit with the four-patch units and the 2½" x 4½" rectangles in horizontal rows. Sew together in rows and press in the direction of the arrows. Join the rows to complete the block. Press.

11. Follow steps 1–10 to make the required number of blocks for the quilt size you are making.

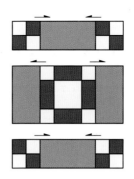

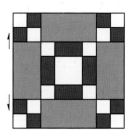

Paducah Nine Patch block

## Assembling the Quilt Top

1. Arrange the blocks on a design wall, evenly distributing the medium and dark blocks throughout the quilt. Sew the blocks together in horizontal rows and press the seams in opposite directions from row to row.

2. Join the rows to complete the quilt top.

## Finishing

1. Layer the quilt top with batting and backing; hand or machine baste the layers together (see page 23).

2. Quilt as desired, bind the edges, add a label, and enjoy your finished quilt.

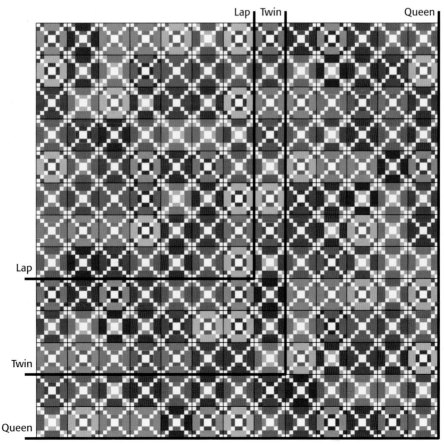

Quilt Plan

# ❧ Mount Hood ❧

*By Pat Speth, 2000, Davenport, Iowa, 75" x 99½".*
*Finished block size: 8"*

You'll notice a wide variety of plaids and prints as well as backgrounds in "Mt. Hood." A flying-geese unit and a six-patch unit make up each block. Varying the placement of the units in the blocks adds interest and motion to the overall effect. Making the pieced border that surrounds the mountains will give you lots of practice making hourglass units.

➴ *Skill level:* Easy

## Quilt Sizes and Statistics

|  | Lap | Twin | Queen |
|---|---|---|---|
| Size | 61" x 68" | 75" x 99½" | 99½ x 106½" |
| Block A | 18 | 40 | 55 |
| Block B | 12 | 30 | 55 |
| Block set | 5 x 6 | 7 x 10 | 10 x 11 |

## Materials

*42"-wide fabric (40" of usable width after preshrinking and removing selvages)*

|  | Lap | Twin | Queen |
|---|---|---|---|
| 5" dark squares | 90 | 183 | 272 |
| 5" light squares | 90 | 183 | 272 |
| Borders and binding | 2 yds. | 2½ yds. | 2⅞ yds. |
| Backing | 3⅞ yds. | 6 yds. | 8⅞ yds. |
| Batting | 65" x 72" | 79" x 104" | 104" x 111" |

## Cutting

*Cut all strips across the fabric width (crosswise grain).*
**Note:** Wait to cut the strips for the inner border until the quilt top is finished. Refer to "Pieced Borders" on page 22.

*Lap Size*

|  | Number of Strips | Strip Width |
|---|---|---|
| Inner border (sides) | 3 | 3¼" |
| Inner border (top and bottom) | 3 | 2¾" |
| Outer border | 6 | 4½" |
| Binding | 7 | 2½" |

*Twin Size*

|  | Number of Strips | Strip Width |
|---|---|---|
| Inner border (sides) | 4 | 2¼" |
| Inner border (top and bottom) | 3 | 2½" |
| Outer border | 9 | 4½" |
| Binding | 10 | 2½" |

*Queen Size*

|  | Number of Strips | Strip Width |
|---|---|---|
| Inner border (sides) | 5 | 2½" |
| Inner border (top and bottom) | 5 | 2" |
| Outer border | 10 | 4½" |
| Binding | 11 | 2½" |

## Making the Blocks

For each block you will need:
    2 different dark 5" squares
    2 different light 5" squares

1. Using 1 dark and 1 light square and referring to "Half-Square-Triangle Units" on page 14, make 2 matching half-square-triangle units and sew together to make 1 flying-geese unit.

Flying-geese unit

2. To make the six-patch unit, place 1 dark and 1 light square right sides together. Stitch opposite edges together using ¼"-wide seams. Cut the resulting unit in half to yield 2 large two-patch units. Press the seam toward the darker fabric.

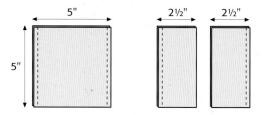

3. *Cutting across the center seam*, trim away ½" from one edge of the first two-patch unit. The resulting unit should measure 4½" x 4½". Cut the second two-patch unit in half across the center seam to yield 2 pieces, each 2½" x 4½".

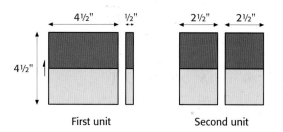

First unit    Second unit

4. Arrange the units from step 3 as shown and sew together to complete the six-patch unit. Press.

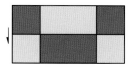

Six-patch unit

5. Arrange the six-patch units and the flying-geese units to make the required number of Mt. Hood A and B blocks for the quilt size you are making (see "Quilt Sizes and Statistics" on page 55).

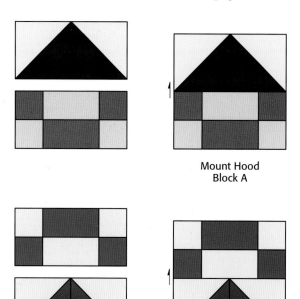

Mount Hood
Block A

Mount Hood
Block B

## Assembling the Quilt Top

Referring to the quilt plan, arrange the blocks in horizontal rows, alternating Block A with Block B in each row and from row to row. Sew the blocks together in horizontal rows and press the seams in opposite directions from row to row.

# Making the Pieced Border

*Pieced-Border Units*

|  | Lap | Twin | Queen |
|---|---|---|---|
| Side border | 15 units per strip | 24 units per strip | 26 units per strip |
| Top and bottom border | 15 units per strip | 19 units per strip | 26 units per strip |
| Total border units | 60 | 86 | 104 |

1. Referring to "Hourglass Units" on page 17, make the required number of hourglass units for the quilt size you are making.

Hourglass unit

2. Alternating the direction of the hourglass units, assemble 2 side pieced-border strips and the top and bottom pieced-border strips required for the quilt size you are making. Sew together and press the seams in one direction.

3. Referring to "Pieced Borders" on page 22, add the inner, pieced, and outer borders to quilt top.

## Finishing

1. Layer the quilt top with batting and backing; hand or machine baste the layers together (see page 23).

2. Quilt as desired, bind the edges, add a label, and enjoy your finished quilt.

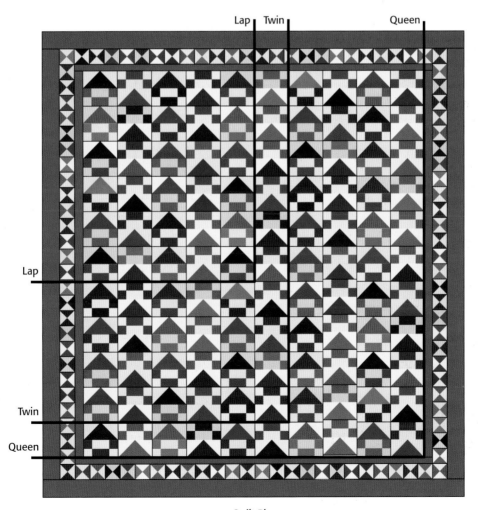

Quilt Plan

# ✻ Tillie's Treasure ✻

*By Pat Speth, 1999, Davenport, Iowa, 73¼" x 94¼".*
*Finished block size: 7"*

*This quilt is lots of fun to make and you'll be amazed at how easy it is. Believe it or not, there are no triangles to cut. Keep it interesting with an assortment of light-colored fabrics— light blues, greens, pinks, and yellows, as well as tans and golds, all make their appearance in "Tillie's Treasure."*

➤ *Skill level:* Easy

## Quilt Sizes and Statistics

|                   | Lap              | Twin             | Queen               |
| ----------------- | ---------------- | ---------------- | ------------------- |
| Size              | 66¼" x 66¼"      | 73¼" x 94¼"      | 101¼" x 101¼"       |
| Number of blocks  | 49               | 88               | 144                 |
| Block set         | 7 x 7            | 8 x 11           | 12 x 12             |

## Materials

*42"-wide fabric (40" of usable width after preshrinking and removing selvages)*

|                                      | Lap                       | Twin                      | Queen                     |
| ------------------------------------ | ------------------------- | ------------------------- | ------------------------- |
| 5" dark squares                      | 49 pairs 16 singles       | 88 pairs 21 singles       | 144 pairs 26 singles      |
| 5" light squares                     | 49 pairs 16 singles       | 88 pairs 21 singles       | 144 pairs 26 singles      |
| Inner and outer borders and binding  | 2⅛ yds.                   | 2⅔ yds.                   | 3⅛ yds.                   |
| Backing                              | 4⅛ yds.                   | 5¾ yds.                   | 9 yds.                    |
| Batting                              | 70" x 70"                 | 77" x 98"                 | 106" x 106"               |

## Cutting

*Cut all strips across the fabric width (crosswise grain).*
**Note:** Wait to cut the strips for the inner border until the quilt top is finished (see "Pieced Borders" on page 22).

### Lap Size

|              | Number of Strips | Strip Width |
| ------------ | ---------------- | ----------- |
| Inner border | 6                | 3⅛"         |
| Outer border | 7                | 4½"         |
| Binding      | 7                | 2½"         |

### Twin Size

|              | Number of Strips | Strip Width |
| ------------ | ---------------- | ----------- |
| Inner border | 7                | 3⅛"         |
| Outer border | 9                | 4½"         |
| Binding      | 9                | 2½"         |

### Queen Size

|              | Nunmber of Strips | Strip Width |
| ------------ | ----------------- | ----------- |
| Inner border | 10                | 3⅛"         |
| Outer border | 10                | 4½"         |
| Binding      | 11                | 2½"         |

# Making the Blocks

For each block you will need:
    1 pair of dark 5" squares
    1 pair of light 5" squares

1. Referring to "Small-Wonders Units" on page 16, use the light and dark squares to make the units shown for each block.

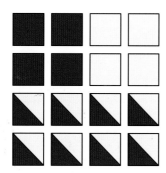

Small-wonders units

2. Arrange the units from step 1 in 4 horizontal rows, paying careful attention to the orientation of each half-square-triangle unit. Sew the units together in each row and press as directed. Join the rows to complete each block. Chain-sew the units together in each row (see page 13) to help keep them in order.

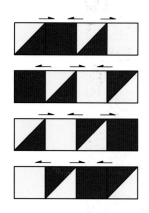

3. Follow steps 1–2 to make the required number of blocks for the quilt size you are making.

# Making the Pieced Border

*Pieced-Border Units*

|  | Lap | Twin | Queen |
|---|---|---|---|
| Side border units | 8 per strip | 12 per strip | 13 per strip |
| Top and bottom border units | 8 per strip | 9 per strip | 13 per strip |
| Total border units | 32 | 42 | 52 |

1. Referring to the directions for the "Small-Wonders Units" on page 16, use the remaining light and dark squares to make the pieced-border units. One dark 5" square and 1 light 5" square will yield the pieces required for 2 border units. Refer to the chart above to determine the number of border units needed for the quilt size you are making.

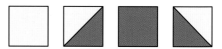

2. For each border unit, arrange a set of the small-wonders units in a horizontal row. Sew the pieces together and press as directed.

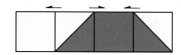

3. Arrange and sew the required number of border units together to form each side and top and bottom border for the quilt size you are making. Press the seams toward the light squares. *Remove the 2¼" light square from one end of each of the pieced side borders and sew to one end of each of the top and bottom borders.*

## Assembling the Quilt Top

1. Referring to the quilt plan for the size you are making, arrange the quilt blocks on your design wall. Sew the blocks together in horizontal rows and press the seams in opposite directions from row to row.

2. Referring to "Pieced Borders" on page 22, add the inner and outer borders to the quilt top.

## Finishing

1. Layer the quilt top with batting and backing; hand or machine baste the layers together (see page 23).

2. Quilt as desired, bind the edges, add a label, and enjoy your finished quilt.

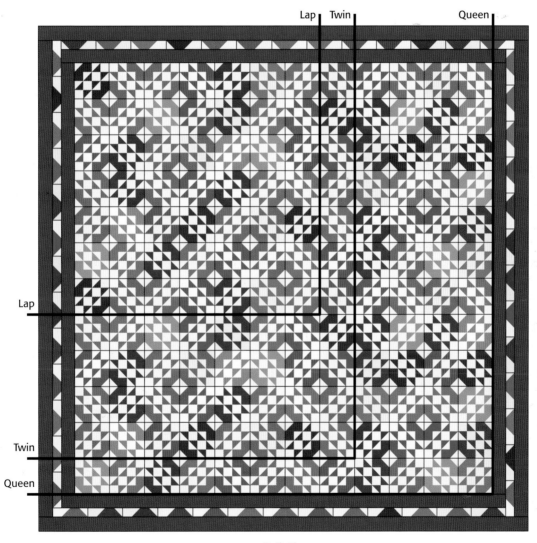

Quilt Plan

# ❧ *Shaded Four Patch* ❧

*By Pat Speth, 1999, Davenport, Iowa, 68½" x 84½".*
*Finished block size: 8"*

*T*wo different blocks made from a large variety of Christmas theme fabrics were used to create this four-patch beauty. There are literally dozens of different ways, other than the one shown here, to set the units to create patterns with these blocks. Be sure to take time to play with the units on a design wall to discover your own variations.

↠ *Skill level:* Easy

## Quilt Sizes and Statistics

|  | Lap | Twin | Queen |
|---|---|---|---|
| Size | 68½" x 84½" | 76½" x 92½" | 100½" x 100½" |
| Block 1 | 36 | 40 | 66 |
| Block 2 | 27 | 40 | 55 |
| Block set | 7 x 9 | 8 x 10 | 11 x 11 |

## Materials

*42"-wide fabric (40" of usable width after preshrinking and removing selvages)*

|  | Lap | Twin | Queen |
|---|---|---|---|
| 5" dark squares | 189 | 240 | 363 |
| Background | 1⅝ yds. | 2 yds. | 3 yds. |
| Inner border | ⅜ yd. | ½ yd. | ½ yd. |
| Outer border and binding | 2 yds. | 2 yds. | 2½ yds. |
| Backing | 5¼ yds. | 5⅝ yds. | 9 yds. |
| Batting | 73" x 89" | 81" x 97" | 105" x 105" |

## Cutting

*Cut all strips across the fabric width (crosswise grain).*

| *Lap Size* | First Cut | | Second Cut | |
|---|---|---|---|---|
|  | Number of Strips | Strip Width | Number of Pieces | Piece Size |
| Background | 16 | 2⅞" | 252 | 2⅞" x 2⅞" ◺ * |
| Inner border | 7 | 1½" | | |
| Outer border | 8 | 5½" | | |
| Binding | 9 | 2½" | | |

| *Twin Size* | First Cut | | Second Cut | |
|---|---|---|---|---|
|  | Number of Strips | Strip Width | Number of Pieces | Piece Size |
| Background | 32 | 2⅞" | 320 | 2⅞" x 2⅞" ◺ * |
| Inner border | 8 | 1½" | | |
| Outer border | 8 | 5½" | | |
| Binding | 9 | 2½" | | |

| *Queen Size* | First Cut | | Second Cut | |
|---|---|---|---|---|
|  | Number of Strips | Strip Width | Number of Pieces | Piece Size |
| Background | 49 | 2⅞" | 484 | 2⅞" x 2⅞" ◺ * |
| Inner border | 10 | 1½" | | |
| Outer border | 10 | 5½" | | |
| Binding | 11 | 2½" | | |

* ◺ = Cut the piece in half diagonally.

# Making the Blocks

Each Shaded Four Patch block requires:
    3 dark 5" squares
    8 background 2½" half-square triangles

1. Trim 2 dark 5" squares to measure 4⅞" x 4⅞" and cut in half on the diagonal to yield 2 half-square triangles each.

2. Cut 1 dark 5" square into 4 squares, each 2½" x 2½". One large square provides enough small squares for 4 shaded four-patch units.

3. Arrange 2 half-square background triangles with a 2½" dark square from step 2. Sew together and press as directed by the arrows.

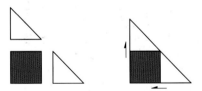

4. Add a dark half-square triangle from step 1 to the long edge of each pieced triangle unit from step 3. Press the seam toward the half-square triangle. You may want to cut several blocks at one time to mix and match for a scrappier look.

5. Repeat steps 1–4 to make 4 shaded four-patch units for each Shaded Four Patch Block 1 and Block 2 required for the quilt size you are making (see "Quilt Sizes and Statistics" on page 63).

6. Arrange the shaded four-patch units in horizontal rows to create the required number of Block 1 and Block 2. Sew the units together in rows. Press. Sew the rows together. Press the seams in the directions of the arrows.

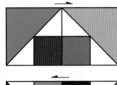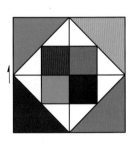
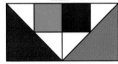

**Shaded Four Patch
Block 1**

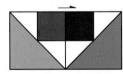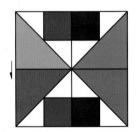
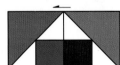

**Shaded Four Patch
Block 2**

## Assembling the Quilt Top

1. Referring to the quilt plan for the size you are making and working on your design wall, arrange Blocks 1 and 2 in alternating fashion to create horizontal rows.

**Note:** For the lap- and queen-size quilts, all rows begin and end with a Block 1. For the twin size, each row begins with a Block 1 and ends with a Block 2.

2. Referring to "Plain Borders" on page 21, add the inner and outer borders to the quilt top.

## Finishing

1. Layer the quilt top with batting and backing; hand or machine baste the layers together (see page 23).

2. Quilt as desired, bind the edges, add a label, and enjoy your finished quilt.

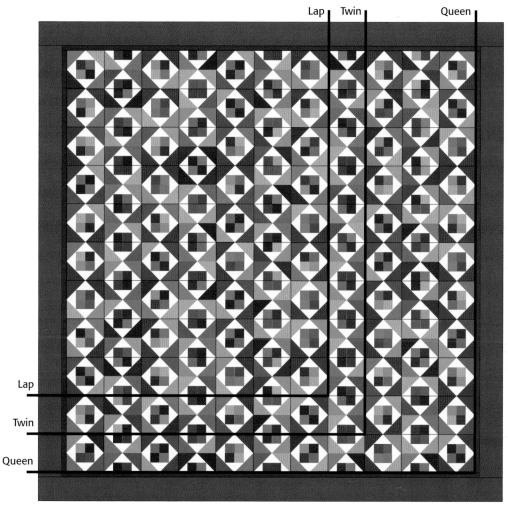

Quilt Plan

# ❋ Morning Star ❋

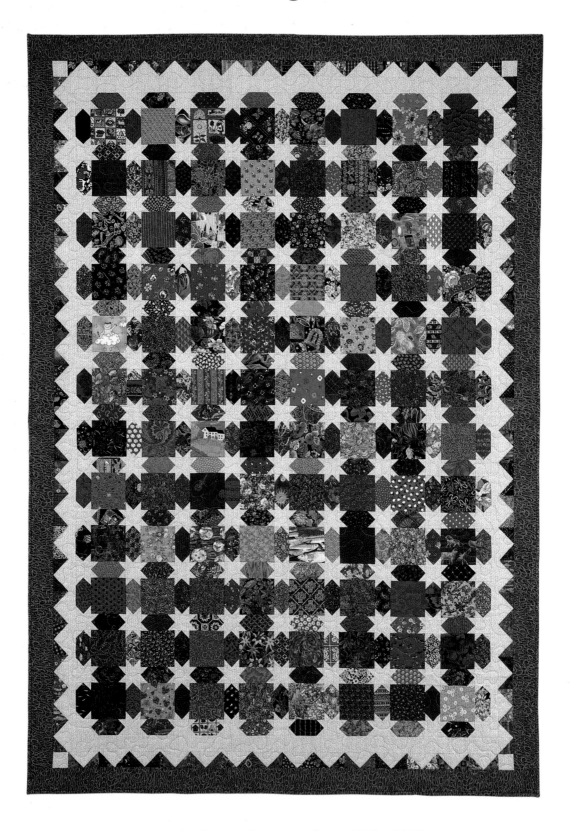

*By Pat Speth, 2001, Davenport, Iowa, 66½" x 94½".*
*Finished block size: 13"*

*If you're looking for a design to feature some of the 5" squares in your collection that are just too pretty to cut up into smaller pieces, this quilt is the perfect candidate. The blocks are easy to assemble using the "Sew and Flip" technique on page 15 to add the small corner triangles.*

→ *Skill level:* Easy

## Quilt Sizes and Statistics

|  | Lap | Twin | Queen |
|---|---|---|---|
| Size | 66½" x 66½" | 66½" x 94½" | 106½" x 106½" |
| Number of blocks | 16 | 24 | 49 |
| Block set | 4 x 4 | 4 x 6 | 7 x 7 |

## Materials

*42"-wide fabric (40" of usable width after preshrinking and removing selvages)*

|  | Lap | Twin | Queen |
|---|---|---|---|
| Assorted 5" squares | 164 | 237 | 454 |
| Background and inner border | 2⅜ yds. | 3⅛ yds. | 5⅜ yds. |
| Outer border and binding | 1⅜ yds. | 1¾ yds. | 2⅛ yds. |
| Backing | 4⅛ yds. | 5¾ yds. | 9½ yds. |
| Batting | 71" x 71" | 71" x 99" | 111" x 111" |

## Cutting

*Cut all strips across the fabric width (crosswise grain).*
**Note:** Wait to cut the strips for the inner border until the quilt top is finished (see "Pieced Borders" on page 22).

### Lap Size

|  | First Cut | | Second Cut | |
|---|---|---|---|---|
|  | Number of Strips | Strip Width | Number of Pieces | Piece Size |
| Background | 23 | 1½" | 576 | 1½" x 1½" |
| Background | 6 | 2½" | 85 | 2½" x 2½" |
| Background | 7 | 2½" | 56 | 2½" x 4½" |
| Inner border | 6 | 1½" | | |
| Outer border | 7 | 3½" | | |
| Binding | 7 | 2½" | | |

### Twin Size

|  | First Cut | | Second Cut | |
|---|---|---|---|---|
|  | Number of Strips | Strip Width | Number of Pieces | Piece Size |
| Background | 33 | 1½" | 848 | 1½" x 1½" |
| Background | 8 | 2½" | 121 | 2½" x 2½" |
| Background | 9 | 2½" | 70 | 2½" x 4½" |
| Inner border (sides) | 4 | 1½" | | |
| Inner border (top and bottom) | 3 | 2½" | | |
| Outer border | 9 | 3½" | | |
| Binding | 9 | 2½" | | |

### Queen Size

|  | First Cut | | Second Cut | |
|---|---|---|---|---|
|  | Number of Strips | Strip Width | Number of Pieces | Piece Size |
| Background | 65 | 1½" | 1680 | 1½" x 1½" |
| Background | 15 | 2½" | 229 | 2½" x 2½" |
| Background | 12 | 2½" | 96 | 2½" x 4½" |
| Inner border | 10 | 2" | | |
| Outer border | 11 | 3½" | | |
| Binding | 12 | 2½" | | |

# Making the Blocks

For each block you will need:
  8 assorted 5" squares
  32 background 1½" squares
  4 background 2½" squares

1. For each block, cut 4 of the 5" squares in half to yield 8 pieces, each 2½" x 5".

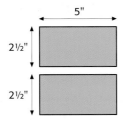

2. Referring to "Sew and Flip" on page 15, sew 2 of the 1½" background squares to opposite corners of each of the 2½" x 5" pieces. Trim and press as shown. Repeat on the remaining opposite corners of each piece. Make 8 for each block.

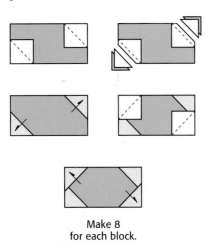

Make 8
for each block.

3. Arrange the units from step 2 with the remaining 5" squares and the 2½" background squares and sew together in horizontal rows. Use chain piecing (see page 13) to keep the pieces in the correct order in each row. Press all seams toward the squares in each row. Sew the rows together to complete the block. Make the required number of blocks for the quilt size you are making. There

will be background and 5" squares left over for steps 5–7, below, and for the pieced borders.

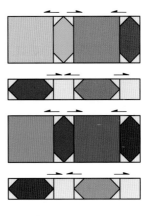

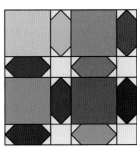

Morning Star block

4. Working on your design wall and referring to the quilt plan and the quilt set (see "Quilt Sizes and Statistics" on page 67), arrange the blocks in the required number of horizontal rows. Sew the blocks together in rows and press the seams in opposite directions from row to row.

5. To complete the design, additional pieced units are required for the upper and left-hand edges of the quilt top. Referring to step 2, make 2 pieced units for each block in the length and width of your quilt. For example, if your quilt set is 4 x 6 (see "Quilt Sizes and Statistics"), you will need 20 units.

6. Sew each set of units together with a 2½" background square between them and another at the end of the resulting unit. Press all seams toward the background squares.

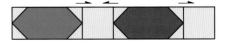

Lap: Make 8.
Twin: Make 20.
Queen: Make 28.

7. Sew the units together to make a strip for the left side of the quilt top. Press the seams toward the background squares and sew the strip to the quilt top. Press. Repeat with the remaining units, adding a 2½" background square at one end to complete the pattern. Press. Sew to the top edge of the quilt top and press.

# Making the Pieced Border

*Pieced-Border Units*

|  | Lap | Twin | Queen |
|---|---|---|---|
| Side | 14 units per strip | 21 units per strip | 24 units per strip |
| Top and bottom | 14 units per strip | 14 units per strip | 24 units per strip |
| Total units | 56 | 70 | 96 |

1. Cut each of the remaining 5" squares into 4 small squares, each 2½" x 2½".

2. Referring to "Flying-Geese Units" on page 20, add 2 squares of matching fabric to each of the 2½" x 4½" background rectangles to make a flying-geese unit. Make the required number for your quilt (see chart above).

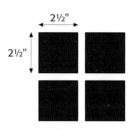

Flying Geese unit

3. Join the flying-geese units in strips as shown to create side and top and bottom borders of the required length for your quilt top (see chart above). Press all seams in each strip in one direction.

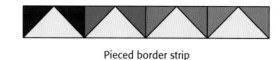

Pieced border strip

# Finishing

1. Referring to "Pieced Borders" on page 22, add the inner, pieced, and outer borders to the quilt top.

2. Layer the quilt top with batting and backing; pin or hand baste the layers together (see page 23).

3. Quilt as desired, bind the edges, add a label, and enjoy your finished quilt.

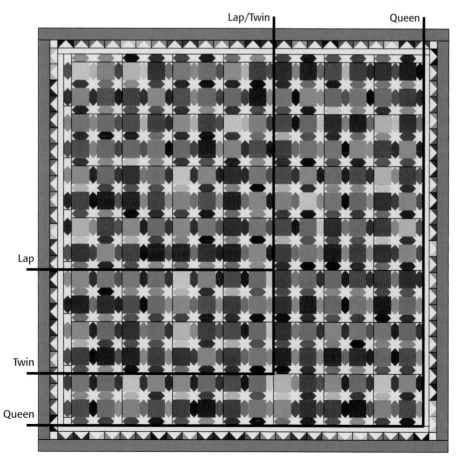

Quilt Plan

# *Flying Home from Bali Bali*

*By Pat Speth, 2000, Davenport, Iowa, 64½" x 96½".*
*Finished block size: 4" x 8"*

*T*his quilt design is a beautiful showcase for a collection of batik fabrics. Flying Geese and simple Eight Patch blocks create the ribbons of color in this easy-to-assemble pattern. Pat carefully arranged the Eight Patch blocks so they flow naturally through the full spectrum of the color wheel. Notice that each column of blocks begins with a different color.

➤ *Skill level:* Easy

## Quilt Sizes and Statistics

|  | Lap | Twin | Queen |
|---|---|---|---|
| Size | 64½" x 64½" | 64½" x 96½" | 104½" x 104½" |
| Flying Geese blocks | 60 | 92 | 176 |
| Eight Patch blocks | 36 | 60 | 110 |
| Block set | 6 x 12 | 6 x 20 | 11 x 22 |

## Materials

*42"-wide fabric (40" of usable width after preshrinking and removing selvages)*

|  | Lap | Twin | Queen |
|---|---|---|---|
| 5" batik squares | 100 | 156 | 290 |
| 5" background squares | 100 | 156 | 290 |
| Inner and outer borders and binding | 1¾ yds. | 2 yds. | 2⅜ yds. |
| Backing | 4⅛ yds. | 5⅞ yds. | 9¼ yds. |
| Batting | 69" x 69" | 69" x 101" | 109" x 109" |

## Cutting

*Cut all strips across the fabric width (crosswise grain).*

*Lap Size*

|  | Number of Strips | Strip Width |
|---|---|---|
| Inner border | 6 | 1½" |
| Outer border | 7 | 3½" |
| Binding | 7 | 2½" |

*Twin Size*

|  | Number of Strips | Strip Width |
|---|---|---|
| Inner border | 7 | 1½" |
| Outer border | 9 | 3½" |
| Binding | 9 | 2½" |

*Queen Size*

|  | Number of Strips | Strip Width |
|---|---|---|
| Inner border | 10 | 1½" |
| Outer border | 10 | 3½" |
| Binding | 11 | 2½" |

## Making the Blocks

For each Flying Geese block, you will need:
    1 batik 5" square
    1 background 5" square

For each Eight Patch block, you will need:
    1 batik 5" square
    1 background 5" square

1. Referring to "Half-Square-Triangle Units" on page 14 and using 1 batik and 1 background square, make 2 identical half-square-triangle units. Press the seam toward the background in one unit and away from the background in the other. Sew the 2 units together to make 1 Flying

Geese block. *Do not press the center joining seam until you have finalized the quilt-top layout (see step 1 in "Assembling the Quilt Top").* Make the required number of Flying Geese blocks for the quilt size you are making (see "Quilt Sizes and Statistics" on page 71). This *includes* the number of flying-geese units required for the borders. In addition, make 4 additional half-square-triangle units for the border corners.

  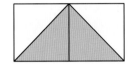

Flying Geese block

2. Referring to the directions for "Four-Patch Units" on page 14 and using 1 batik square and 1 background square, make 2 four-patch units. Sew the units together to make 1 Eight Patch block. *Do not press the center joining seam* until you have finalized the quilt-top layout (see step 1, below). Make the required number of Eight Patch blocks for the quilt size you are making.

Eight Patch block

## Assembling the Quilt Top

1. Working on your design wall and referring to the quilt plan and photo, arrange the Flying Geese and Eight Patch blocks in columns. Plan the color placement to follow the spectrum of the color wheel if desired, beginning each column of Eight Patch blocks with a different color. Press the center seams in the Flying Geese and Eight Patch blocks in alternating directions down the column.

2. Sew the blocks together in vertical columns to create strips of Flying Geese and strips of Eight Patch blocks. Press the joining seams in the geese strips toward the points; press the joining seams in the Eight Patch strips in the opposite direction.

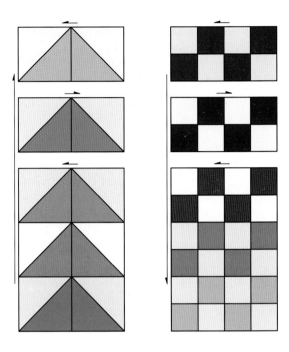

## Making the Pieced Border

*Pieced-Border Blocks*

|  | Lap | Twin | Queen |
| --- | --- | --- | --- |
| Sides | 6 per strip | 10 per strip | 11 per strip |
| Top and bottom | 6 per strip | 6 per strip | 11 per strip |
| Total flying-geese blocks | 24 | 32 | 44 |

1. Using the Flying Geese blocks you made earlier, assemble the pieced-border strips. Refer to the chart above to determine how many blocks to use for each border strip. Sew the blocks together in each strip and press the seams in one direction.

2. Referring to "Pieced Borders" on page 22, measure, cut, and assemble the side inner-border strips. Sew a side inner-border strip to each side pieced-border strip, taking care to sew it to the edge ncarest the points in the Flying Geese blocks. Sew the combined inner- and pieced-border strips to opposite sides of the quilt top. Press the seams toward the inner-border strips.

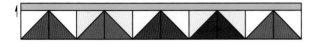

3. From a 1½"-wide strip of inner-border fabric, cut 4 spacer strips, each 1½" x 4½". Sew a spacer strip to each end of the top and bottom pieced-border strips. Add a half-square-triangle unit (from step 1 in "Making the Blocks") to each end of the top and bottom pieced strips. Press seams toward the spacer strips.

4. Cut and add inner-border strips to the top and bottom pieced-border strips as you did for the side pieced-border strips. Sew the combined inner- and pieced-border strips to the top and bottom edges of the quilt top. Press the seams toward the inner-border strips.

5. Referring to "Plain Borders" on page 21, add the outer border to the quilt top.

## Finishing

1. Layer the quilt top with batting and backing; pin or hand baste the layers together (see page 23).

2. Quilt as desired, bind the edges, add a label, and enjoy your finished quilt.

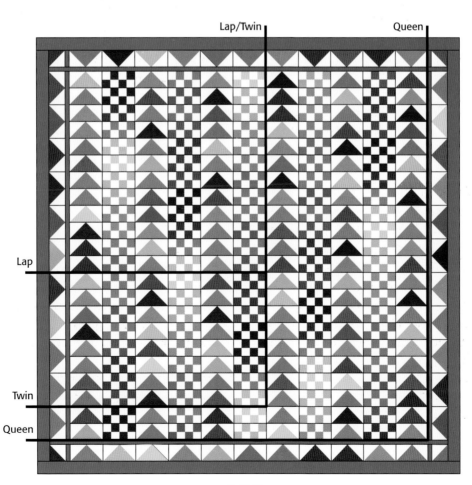

Quilt Plan

# Pinwheel

*By Robin Korth, 2000, Davenport, Iowa, 60" x 79".*
*Finished block size: 7½"*

*P*inwheel and its sister quilt, "Labor Day Madness," shown on page 78, are made from combination units (see page 17). You can make both of these quilts at the same time because "Pinwheel" is made from the right-sided combination units and "Labor Day Madness" is made from the left-sided units. Make one to give as a gift for a special occasion and keep the other for yourself.

The fabric yardage for the blocks' main and background fabrics is enough for two quilts. For a "lodge" look like the one shown, select fabric squares in a variety of prints and plaids and use assorted background fabrics instead of just one.

➤ *Skill level:* Easy

## Quilt Sizes and Statistics

|  | Lap | Twin | Queen |
|---|---|---|---|
| Size | 60" x 79" | 79" x 98" | 107½" x 107½" |
| Number of blocks | 35 | 63 | 100 |
| Block set | 5 x 7 | 7 x 9 | 10 x 10 |

## Materials

*42"-wide fabric (40" of usable width after preshrinking and removing selvages)*

|  | Lap | Twin | Queen |
|---|---|---|---|
| 5" dark squares | 35 sets of 2<br>35 sets of 4 | 63 sets of 2<br>63 sets of 4 | 100 sets of 2<br>100 sets of 4 |
| 5" background squares | 35 sets of 2 | 63 sets of 2 | 100 sets of 2 |
| 5" squares of assorted background colors for cornerstones | 12 | 20 | 31 |
| Sashing | 1⅜ yds. | 2¼ yds. | 3¼ yds. |
| Inner border | ⅜ yd. | ½ yd. | ½ yd. |
| Outer border and binding | 1⅝ yds. | 2 yds. | 2⅜ yds. |
| Backing | 3⅞ yds. | 5⅞ yds. | 9⅝ yds. |
| Batting | 64" x 83" | 83" x 102" | 112" x 112" |

## Cutting

*Cut all strips across the fabric width (crosswise grain).*

| *Lap Size* | First Cut | | Second Cut | |
|---|---|---|---|---|
|  | Number of Strips | Strip Width | Number of Pieces | Piece Size |
| Sashing | 17 | 2½" | 82 | 2½" x 8" |
| Inner border | 7 | 1½" | | |
| Outer border | 7 | 4½" | | |
| Binding | 8 | 2½" | | |

| *Twin Size* | First Cut | | Second Cut | |
|---|---|---|---|---|
|  | Number of Strips | Strip Width | Number of Pieces | Piece Size |
| Sashing | 29 | 2½" | 142 | 2½" x 8" |
| Inner border | 9 | 1½" | | |
| Outer border | 9 | 4½" | | |
| Binding | 10 | 2½" | | |

| *Queen Size* | First Cut | | Second Cut | |
|---|---|---|---|---|
|  | Number of Strips | Strip Width | Number of Pieces | Piece Size |
| Sashing | 44 | 2½" | 220 | 2½" x 8" |
| Inner border | 10 | 1½" | | |
| Outer border | 11 | 4½" | | |
| Binding | 12 | 2½" | | |

# Making the Blocks

For each block you will need:
 1 set of 2 dark 5" squares
 1 set of 2 background 5" squares
 1 set of 4 dark 5" squares

1. Using 2 dark 5" squares (for small triangles) and 2 background 5" squares, make combination units as directed in steps 1–5 on page 17.

2. At step 6 on page 17, add the 4 dark 5" squares (for large triangles) to complete the units, yielding a total of 8 combination units. Four of the units will be right-sided units and the remaining 4 will be left-sided units. *Set aside the left-sided units for the "Labor Day Madness" quilt on page 78.*

Left-sided
combination unit

Right-sided
combination unit

3. Arrange the right-sided combination units in 2 rows of 2 units, making sure to position them so the large triangle rotates positions around the block. Sew the units together in rows and press the seams in opposite directions. Sew the rows together to complete the block. Press the seam in one direction. Make the required number of Pinwheel blocks for the quilt size you are making.

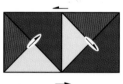

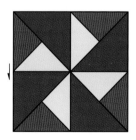

Pinwheel block

# Assembling the Quilt Top

1. Cut the assorted background squares into 2½" squares for the cornerstones.

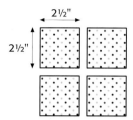

2½"

2½"

2. Referring to the quilt plan and working on your design wall, arrange the Pinwheel blocks in horizontal rows with 2½" x 8" sashing strips in between the blocks and at each end of each row. Arrange the horizontal sashing strips between each row, beginning and ending with a cornerstone. Sew the pieces together in horizontal rows and press all seams toward the sashing strips.

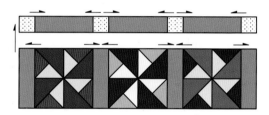

3. Sew the rows and sashing strips together to complete the quilt top. Press the seams in one direction.

4. Referring to "Plain Borders" on page 21, add the inner and outer borders to the quilt top.

# Finishing

1. Layer the quilt top with batting and backing; pin or hand baste the layers together (see page 23).

2. Quilt as desired, bind the edges, add a label, and enjoy your finished quilt.

Lap

Twin

Queen

Lap

Twin

Queen

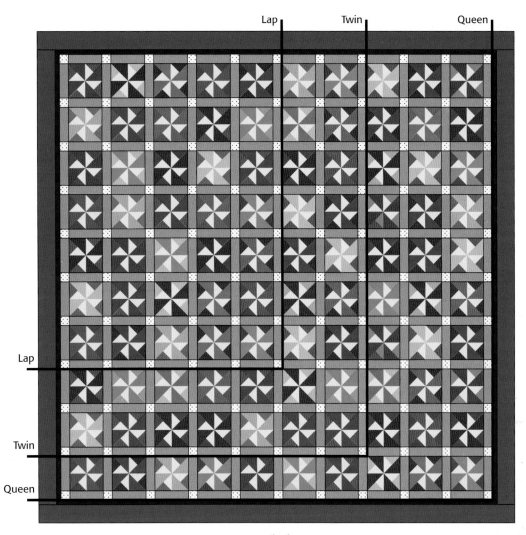

Quilt Plan

# ✻ Labor Day Madness ✻

*By Robin Korth, 1999, Davenport, Iowa, 70¼" x 88½".*
*Finished block size: 9⅜"*

*I*t's really fun to make two quilts at the same time, and it's easy when you make the combination units for "Labor Day Madness" because the process also yields enough for the blocks in "Pinwheel" on page 74. "Labor Day Madness" requires the left-sided combination units and "Pinwheel" the right-sided combination units.

The fabric requirements for the block's main fabric and background fabrics is enough to make the blocks for both quilts. If you've already made "Pinwheel," you're ready to assemble the blocks for this quilt.

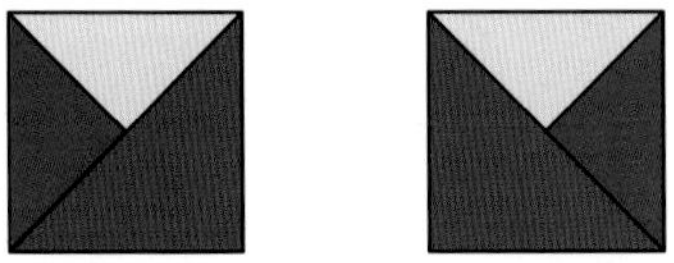

| Left-sided combination unit | Right-sided combination unit |

➤ *Skill level:* Intermediate

## Quilt Sizes and Statistics

|  | Lap | Twin | Queen |
|---|---|---|---|
| Size | 60½" x 60½" | 70¼" x 88½" | 98½" x 106½" |
| Number of blocks | 16 | 35 | 72 |
| Block set | 4 x 4 | 5 x 7 | 8 x 9 |

## Materials:

*42"-wide fabric (40" of usable width after preshrinking and removing selvages)*

|  | Lap | Twin | Queen |
|---|---|---|---|
| 5" dark squares | 16 sets of 2<br>16 sets of 4 | 35 sets of 2<br>35 sets of 4 | 72 sets of 2<br>72 sets of 4 |
| 5" background squares | 16 sets of 5 | 35 sets of 5 | 72 sets of 5 |
| 5" assorted main-fabric squares | 46 | 65 | 88 |

*continued*

*Materials continued*

|  | Lap | Twin | Queen |
|---|---|---|---|
| 5" background fabric squares | 46 | 65 | 88 |
| Borders and binding | 2 yds. | 2⅔ yds. | 3¼ yds. |
| Backing | 3⅞ yds. | 5⅜ yds. | 8¾ yds. |
| Batting | 65" x 65" | 75" x 93" | 103" x 111" |

## Cutting

*Cut all strips across the fabric width (crosswise grain).*

**Note:** Wait to cut the strips for the inner border until the quilt top is finished. Refer to "Pieced Borders" on page 22.

*Lap Size*

|  | Number of Strips | Strip Width |
|---|---|---|
| Inner border | 5 | 2¾" |
| Outer border | 6 | 5½" |
| Binding | 7 | 2½" |

*Twin Size*

|  | Number of Strips | Strip Width |
|---|---|---|
| Inner border (sides) | 4 | 3" |
| Inner border (top and bottom) | 3 | 2¾" |
| Outer border | 8 | 5½" |
| Binding | 9 | 2½" |

*Queen Size*

|  | Number of Strips | Strip Width |
|---|---|---|
| Inner border (sides) | 5 | 3" |
| Inner border (top and bottom) | 4 | 2⅜" |
| Outer border | 10 | 5½" |
| Binding | 11 | 2½" |

## Making the Blocks

For each block you will need:
- 1 set of 2 dark 5" squares
- 1 set of 5 background 5" squares
- 1 set of 4 dark 5" squares

1. Using the 2 dark 5" squares (for small triangles) and 2 background 5" squares, make combination units as directed in steps 1–5 on page 17.

2. At step 6 on page 17, add the 4 dark squares (for large triangles), yielding a total of 8 combination units. Four of the units will be right-sided units and the remaining 4 will be left-sided units. Four left-sided units make 1 block. *Set aside the right-sided units for the "Pinwheel" quilt on page 74.*

Left-sided
combination unit

3. Cut each of 2 of the remaining 5" background squares into 2 rectangles, each 2⅜" x 4½", for a total of 4 rectangles. From the remaining background square, cut 1 square, 2⅜" x 2⅜". Sew 1 background rectangle to each of the combination units as shown. Press the seam toward the rectangle.

Make 4
for each block.

4. To avoid sewing any seams with inside corners, you will sew a partial seam to join the units to complete the block. Sew the 2⅜" background square to one combination unit, stopping halfway as shown. Press the seam away from the square.

5. Add the remaining units in the order shown and press as directed. Complete the partial seam after adding the last combination unit.

Labor Day Madness block

6. Follow steps 1–5 to make the required number of blocks for the quilt size you are making.

## Making the Pieced Border

*Pieced-Border Units*

|  | Lap | Twin | Queen |
|---|---|---|---|
| Side borders | 21 per strip | 35 per strip | 44 per strip |
| Top and bottom borders | 25 per strip | 30 per strip | 44 per strip |
| Total border units | 92 | 130 | 176 |

1. Referring to "Flying-Geese Units" on page 20, make the required number of units for the quilt size you are making (see chart above). Use the 5" main-fabric squares and the individual 5" background squares.

Flying-geese unit

2. Sew the border units together in strips of the required number for each border strip (see chart above). Press toward the triangle points.

## Assembling the Quilt Top

1. Referring to the quilt plan and working on your design wall, arrange the blocks in horizontal rows. Sew the blocks together in rows and press the seams in opposite directions from row to row.

2. Referring to "Pieced Borders" on page 22, add the inner, pieced, and outer borders to quilt top.

## Finishing

1. Layer the quilt top with batting and backing; hand or machine baste the layers together (see page 23).

2. Quilt as desired, bind the edges, add a label, and enjoy your finished quilt.

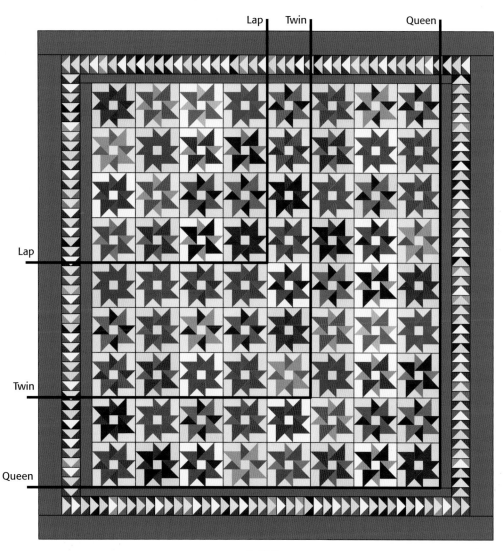

Quilt Plan

# Ozark Maple Leaf

*By Pat Speth, 2000, Davenport, Iowa, 74½" x 98½".*
*Finished block size: 12"*

*H*ere's another perfect quilt design for showcasing batik fabrics. Try it in jewel tones or traditional autumn colors. Use a variety of background fabrics to make it easy to create the tessellated design.

↠ *Skill level:* Intermediate

## Quilt Sizes and Statistics

|                    | Lap              | Twin             | Queen              |
| ------------------ | ---------------- | ---------------- | ------------------ |
| Size               | 62½" x 62½"      | 74½" x 98½"      | 102½" x 102½"      |
| Number of blocks   | 16               | 35               | 49                 |
| Block set          | 4 x 4            | 5 x 7            | 7 x 7              |

## Materials

*42"-wide fabric (40" of usable width after preshrinking and removing selvages)*

|                                          | Lap          | Twin         | Queen        |
| ---------------------------------------- | ------------ | ------------ | ------------ |
| 5" background squares (assorted singles) | 19           | 22           | 21           |
| 5" batik squares                         | 32 sets of 3 | 70 sets of 3 | 98 sets of 3 |
| 5" background squares                    | 32 sets of 3 | 70 sets of 3 | 98 sets of 3 |
| 5" batik squares (assorted singles)      | 19           | 22           | 21           |
| Inner and outer borders and binding      | 1⅔ yds.      | 2⅜ yds.      | 3¼ yds.      |
| Backing                                  | 4 yds.       | 6 yds.       | 9⅛ yds.      |
| Batting                                  | 67" x 67"    | 79" x 103"   | 107" x 107"  |

## Cutting

*Cut all strips across the fabric width (crosswise grain).*
**Note:** Wait to cut the strips for the inner border until the quilt top is finished. Refer to "Pieced Borders" on page 22.

*Lap Size*

|              | Number of Strips | Strip Width |
| ------------ | ---------------- | ----------- |
| Inner border | 6                | 2½"         |
| Outer border | 6                | 3½"         |
| Binding      | 7                | 2½"         |

*Twin Size*

|              | Number of Strips | Strip Width |
| ------------ | ---------------- | ----------- |
| Inner border | 9                | 2½"         |
| Outer border | 9                | 3½"         |
| Binding      | 10               | 2½"         |

*Queen Size*

|              | Number of Strips | Strip Width |
| ------------ | ---------------- | ----------- |
| Inner border | 10               | 2½"         |
| Outer border | 10               | 5½"         |
| Binding      | 11               | 2½"         |

## Making the Blocks

For each block you will need:
  2 sets of 3 batik 5" squares
  2 sets of 3 background 5" squares

1. To begin construction, select 4 assorted background squares; cut into 2½" x 2½" squares and set aside. This pile will be the "kitty" and will always consist of 2½" background squares.

2. Match each set of 3 batik squares with 1 set of 3 background squares, to create 6 pairs.

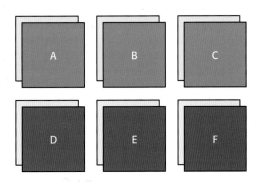

3. Trim ½" from the adjacent sides of both squares in pair A so they measure 4½" x 4½".

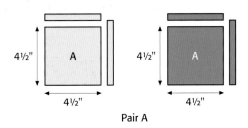

Pair A

4. Trim ½" from one side of each square in pair B. In the opposite direction, cut the pair in half to yield 4 pieces, each 2½" x 4½".

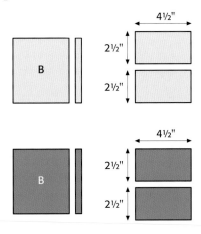

Pair B

5. Cut pair C into 2½" squares. You will use 3 of the resulting batik squares and 1 background square to make the block. Set aside 1 batik and 1 background square to use in the border. Add the remaining 2 background squares to the kitty.

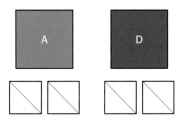

Pair C

6. Repeat steps 3–5 with pairs D, E, and F.

7. From the kitty, select 2 pairs of 2½" squares; try not to repeat the 2 backgrounds you already have for the block. Draw a diagonal line on the wrong side of both pairs of background squares. You will sew them to the 4½" batik squares (pieces A and D from step 2) in step 8.

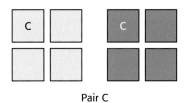

8. With right sides together, place each pair of 2½" background squares at opposite corners of the batik 4½" squares. Stitch, referring to "Sew and Flip" on page 15. Stitch the waste triangles if desired. Press the seams toward the triangles.

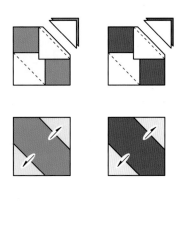

9. From the 2 sets of 3 batik 2½" squares, draw a diagonal line on the wrong side of 2 squares from each set. With right sides together, place 1 batik square from each pair at opposite corners of each background 4½" square as shown. Stitch referring to "Sew and Flip" on page 15. Stitch the waste triangles if desired.

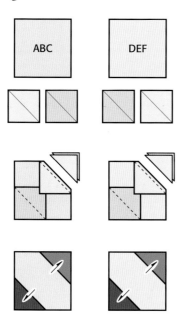

10. Arrange the units from steps 8 and 9 with the rectangles and the remaining 2½" batik and background squares to make the block. Sew together in horizontal rows and press in the direction of the arrows.

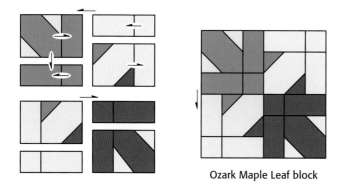

Ozark Maple Leaf block

11. Repeat steps 1–10 to make the required number of blocks for the quilt size you are making.

# Making the Pieced Border
## *Pieced-Border Units*

|  | Lap | Twin | Queen |
|---|---|---|---|
| Sides | 26 per strip | 44 per strip | 44 per strip |
| Top and bottom borders | 28 per strip | 34 per strip | 46 per strip |
| Total units | 108 | 156 | 180 |

1. For each border unit required (see chart above), place 1 background 2½" square and 1 batik 2½" square right sides together (see step 5 in "Making the Blocks"). Stitch, following the "Sew and Flip" method on page 15. Stitch the waste triangles if desired. Press the seams toward the darker triangles.

2. Assemble the pieced-border strips with the required number of units in each one, alternating the direction of the diagonal seams. Press seams in one direction.

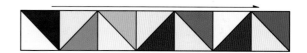

## Assembling the Quilt Top

1. Referring to the quilt plan and working on your design wall, arrange the blocks in horizontal rows. Sew the blocks together in rows and press the seams in opposite directions from row to row.

2. Referring to "Pieced Borders" on page 22, add the inner, pieced, and outer borders to quilt top.

## Finishing

1. Layer the quilt top with batting and backing; hand or machine baste the layers together (see page 23).

2. Quilt as desired, bind the edges, add a label, and enjoy your finished quilt.

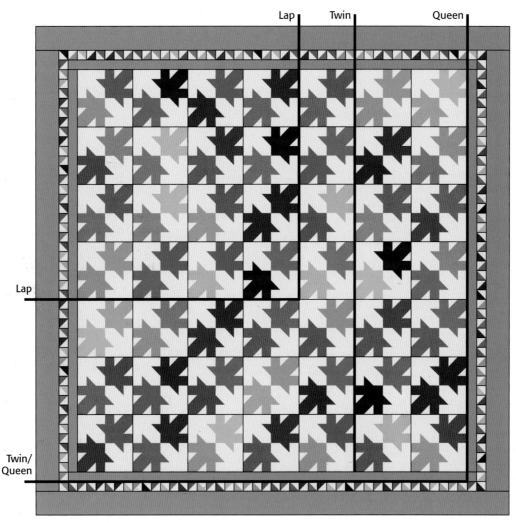

Quilt Plan

# Buffalo Ridge

*By Pat Speth, 2001, Davenport, Iowa, 78½" x 94½".*
*Finished block size: 14"*

A large assortment of plaids and prints set against a tan-plaid background make this a visually active quilt. Tone-on-tone prints were used for the strips in the block centers and look like solids from a distance.

→ *Skill level:* Intermediate

## Quilt Sizes and Statistics

|  | Lap | Twin | Queen |
|---|---|---|---|
| Size | 66½" x 66½" | 78½" x 94½" | 106½" x 106½" |
| Number of blocks | 9 | 20 | 36 |
| Block set | 3 x 3 | 4 x 5 | 6 x 6 |

## Materials:

*42"-wide fabric (40" of usable width after preshrinking and removing selvages)*

|  | Lap | Twin | Queen |
|---|---|---|---|
| 5" print squares | 62 | 116 | 190 |
| Background | 1⅝ yds. | 2½ yds. | 3⅔ yds. |
| 5" plaid squares | 62 | 116 | 190 |
| Center strips* ⅛-yd. cuts (1 per block) | 9 (1⅛ yds. total) | 20 (2½ yds. total) | 36 (4½ yds. total) |
| Inner border | ¾ yd. | ¾ yd. | ⅞ yd. |
| Outer border and binding | 1¾ yds. | 2⅓ yds. | 2¾ yds. |
| Backing | 4¼ yds. | 5¾ yds. | 9½ yds. |
| Batting | 71" x 71" | 83" x 99" | 111" x 111" |

*\* Use a different tone-on-tone for each block.*

## Cutting

*Cut all strips across the fabric width (crosswise grain).*
**Note:** Wait to cut the strips for the inner border until the quilt top is finished (see directions for pieced borders on page 22).

| Lap Size | First Cut | | Second Cut | |
|---|---|---|---|---|
|  | Number of Strips | Strip Width | Number of Pieces | Piece Size |
| Background | 14 | 2½" | 217 | 2½" x 2½" |
| Background | 6 | 2⅞" | 72 | 2⅞" x 2⅞" ◻* |
| Tone-on-tone print | 1 of each fabric | 2½" | 4 | 2½" x 6½" |
| Inner border | 6 | 3½" |  |  |
| Outer border | 7 | 5½" |  |  |
| Binding | 8 | 2½" |  |  |

| Twin Size | First Cut | | Second Cut | |
|---|---|---|---|---|
|  | Number of Strips | Strip Width | Number of Pieces | Piece Size |
| Background | 20 | 2½" | 308 | 2½" x 2½" |
| Background | 12 | 2⅞" | 160 | 2⅞" x 2⅞" ◻* |
| Tone-on-tone print | 1 of each fabric | 2½" | 4 | 2½" x 6½" |
| Inner border (sides) | 4 | 2½" |  |  |
| Inner border (top and bottom) | 3 | 3½" |  |  |
| Outer border | 9 | 5½" |  |  |
| Binding | 10 | 2½" |  |  |

*\* ◻ = Cut piece in half diagonally.*

| Queen Size | First Cut | | Second Cut | |
|---|---|---|---|---|
| | Number of Strips | Strip Width | Number of Pieces | Piece Size |
| Background | 26 | 2½" | 404 | 2½" x 2½" |
| Background | 21 | 2⅞" | 288 | 2⅞" x 2⅞" ◻ * |
| Tone-on-tone print | 1 of each fabric | 2½" | 4 | 2½" x 6½" |
| Inner border | 10 | 2½" | | |
| Outer border | 11 | 5½" | | |
| Binding | 12 | 2½" | | |

* ◻ = *Cut piece in half diagonally.*

## Making the Blocks

For each block you will need:
  4 print 5" squares
  16 background half-square triangles
  4 plaid 5" squares
  4 tone-on-tone print 2½" x 6½" pieces
  1 background 2½" square

1. Cut each 5" print square into 4 squares, each 2½" x 2½". Set aside 1 small square from each print. You will use only 3 small squares from each larger square you cut. Arrange each set of 3 squares with background half-square triangles in horizontal rows and sew together. Press all seams toward the squares. Sew the rows together and press as directed.

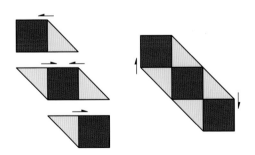

2. Trim the 4 plaid 5" squares to measure 4⅞" x 4⅞" and cut in half on the diagonal. Sew the plaid half-square triangles to the units from step 1.

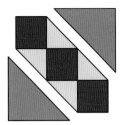

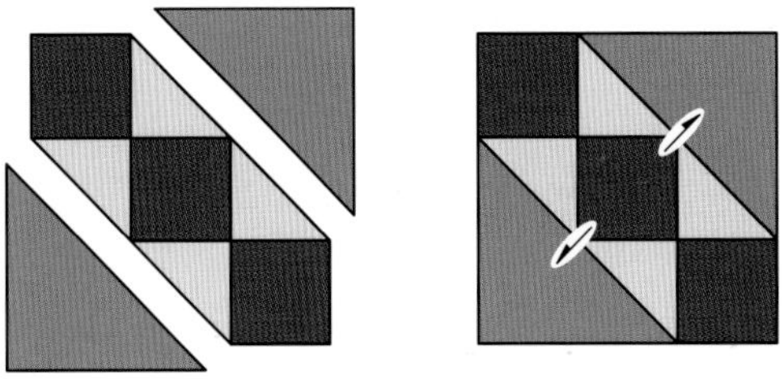

Make 4
for each block.

3. Arrange the 4 pieced units from step 2 in horizontal rows with 4 tone-on-tone strips and a 2½" background square. Sew the pieces together in rows and press all seams toward the tone-on-tone strips. Sew the rows together to complete the Buffalo Ridge block.

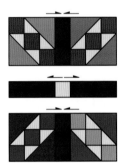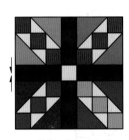

Buffalo Ridge block

4. Repeat steps 1–3 to make the required number of blocks for the quilt size you are making.

## Making the Pieced Border

*Pieced-Border Blocks*

| | Lap | Twin | Queen |
|---|---|---|---|
| Side | 12 per strip | 19 per strip | 22 per strip |
| Top and bottom | 14 per strip | 17 per strip | 24 per strip |
| Total border units | 208 | 288 | 368 |
| Total border blocks | 104 | 144 | 184 |

1. Referring to "Flying-Geese Units" on page 20 and using the remaining assorted plaid and print 5" squares, make the required number of border units for the quilt size you are making.

2. Sew the units together in pairs to make each border block required.

Flying-geese
border block

3. Arrange the required number of blocks for each border strip, alternating the direction of the points along the length of each border strip. Sew together and press seams in one direction.

## Assembling the Quilt Top

1. Referring to the quilt plan and working on your design wall, arrange the blocks in horizontal rows. Sew the blocks together in rows and press the seams in opposite directions from row to row.

2. Referring to "Pieced Borders" on page 22, add the inner, pieced, and outer borders to quilt top.

## Finishing

1. Layer the quilt top with batting and backing; hand or machine baste the layers together (see page 23).

2. Quilt as desired, bind the edges, add a label, and enjoy your finished quilt.

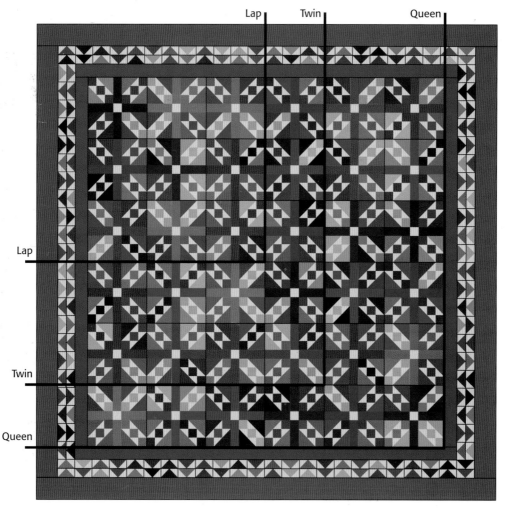

Quilt Plan

# ✷ *Dutchman's Puzzle* ✷

*By Pat Speth, 1999, Davenport, Iowa, 69" x 83".*
*Finished block size: 8"*

*D*utchman's Puzzle blocks are made from flying-geese units that are sewn together in pairs. The points rotate around the blocks, creating lots of motion in the quilt top. Since each pair of flying-geese units requires only one light and one dark 5" square, this quilt provides an opportunity to use up 5" squares that have no mates in your collection. The colorful, scrappy blocks are set on point with a scrappy sashing to make a really fun and visually interesting quilt.

→ *Skill level:* Intermediate

## Quilt Sizes and Statistics

|  | Lap | Twin | Queen |
|---|---|---|---|
| Size | 55" x 69" | 69" x 83" | 97" x 97" |
| Number of blocks | 18 | 32 | 61 |
| Diagonal block set | 3 x 4 | 4 x 5 | 6 x 6 |

## Materials

*42"-wide fabric (40" of usable width after preshrinking and removing selvages)*

|  | Lap | Twin | Queen |
|---|---|---|---|
| Assorted 5" squares | 72 | 128 | 244 |
| Background | 2⅛ yds. | 3⅜ yds. | 5⅝ yds. |
| Sashing—assorted fabrics to total | 1 yd. | 1⅝ yds. | 2¾ yds. |
| Inner border | ⅜ yd. | ⅜ yd. | ½ yd. |
| Outer border and binding | 1¾ yds. | 2 yds. | 2½ yds. |
| Backing | 3½ yds. | 5⅛ yds. | 8⅔ yds. |
| Batting | 59" x 73" | 73" x 87" | 101" x 101" |

## Cutting

*Lap Size*

|  | First Cut | | Second Cut | |
|---|---|---|---|---|
|  | Number of Strips | Strip Width | Number of Pieces | Piece Size |
| Background | 20 | 2½" | 319 | 2½" x 2½" |
| Background | 1 | 12⅝" | 3 | 12⅝" x 12⅝" |
| Background | 1 | 6⅝" | 2 | 6⅝" x 6⅝" |
| Inner border | 6 | 1½" |  |  |
| Outer border | 7 | 5½" |  |  |
| Binding | 7 | 2½" |  |  |

*Twin Size*

|  | First Cut | | Second Cut | |
|---|---|---|---|---|
|  | Number of Strips | Strip Width | Number of Pieces | Piece Size |
| Background | 36 | 2½" | 561 | 2½" x 2½" |
| Background | 2 | 12⅝" | 4 | 12⅝" x 12⅝" |
|  |  |  | 2 | 6⅝" x 6⅝" |
| Inner border | 7 | 1½" |  |  |
| Outer border | 8 | 5½" |  |  |
| Binding | 8 | 2½" |  |  |

*Queen Size*

|  | First Cut | | Second Cut | |
|---|---|---|---|---|
|  | Number of Strips | Strip Width | Number of Pieces | Piece Size |
| Background | 67 | 2½" | 1060 | 2½" x 2½" |
| Background | 2 | 12⅝" | 5 | 12⅝" x 12⅝" |
|  |  |  | 2 | 6⅝" x 6⅝" |
| Inner border | 10 | 1½" |  |  |
| Outer border | 10 | 5½" |  |  |
| Binding | 11 | 2½" |  |  |

## Cutting the Sashing

1. For all quilt sizes, cut 2½"-wide strips from the assorted sashing fabrics.

2. Crosscut into the required number of 2½" x 8½" strips for the quilt size you are making:

   Lap      48
   Twin     80
   Queen    144

   If you prefer, you can cut and piece the sashing from 5" squares in your collection. Cut each square in half and sew the resulting 2½" x 5" pieces together end to end. Press the seam open and trim to 2½" x 8½".

## Making the Blocks

For each block you will need:
   4 assorted dark 5" squares
   16 background 2½" squares

1. Referring to "Flying-Geese Units" on page 20, use 4 assorted 5" squares and 16 background 2½" squares to make a total of 8 flying-geese units for each block. Sew together in pairs.

Make 4 pairs.

2. Arrange and sew the 4 units together in 2 rows. Sew the rows together to complete the block. Press in direction of the arrows.

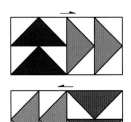 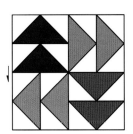

Dutchman's Puzzle block

3. Repeat steps 1 and 2 to make the required number of blocks for the quilt size you are making.

## Assembling the Quilt Top

1. Cut the 6⅝" background squares once diagonally to yield 4 corner triangles.

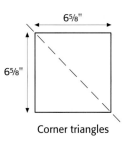

Corner triangles

2. Refer to the cutting chart for the number of 12⅝" squares needed for the side setting triangles for your quilt size. Cut the squares twice diagonally.

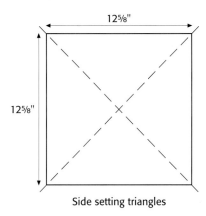

Side setting triangles

3. Working on your design wall and referring to the quilt plan for the size you are making, arrange the blocks and setting triangles in a diagonal set with the sashing strips and the remaining 2½" background squares. Sew the sashing squares and strips together in rows. Press the seams toward the sashing strips.

4. Sew the side setting triangles and blocks together in diagonal rows with the 2½" x 8½" sashing strips between the blocks. Press all seams toward the sashing strips. Add the corner triangles and press the seams toward the sashing.

**Note:** The side setting and corner triangles are oversized; you will trim to the correct size *after* the quilt top is assembled. Refer to the illustration below for the correct positioning of each triangle for stitching.

5. Join the rows and press. Using a ruler and rotary cutter, trim the excess from the setting triangles, *leaving a ¼"-wide seam allowance beyond the outer points of the sashing strips.*

6. Add the inner and outer borders, referring to "Plain Borders" on page 21.

## Finishing

1. Layer the quilt top with batting and backing; hand or machine baste the layers together (see page 23).

2. Quilt as desired, bind the edges, add a label, and enjoy your finished quilt.

Lap-Size Quilt Plan

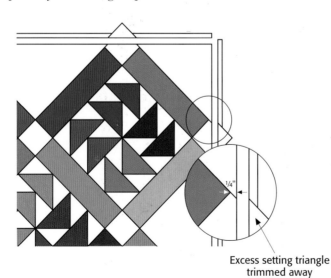

¼"

Excess setting triangle
trimmed away

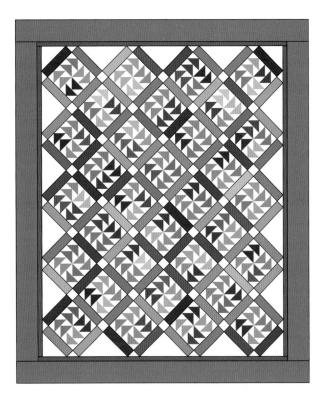

Twin-Size Quilt Plan

Queen-Size Quilt Plan

# ❧ *All That Glitters* ❧

*By Pat Speth, 1999, Davenport, Iowa, 63½" x 77½".*
*Finished block size: 14"*

*T*his quilt radiates with star energy and is a lot easier to make than it looks. We combined plaids and prints of dark and medium values with a variety of background fabrics for a wonderful scrappy look.

→ *Skill level:* Intermediate

## Quilt Sizes and Statistics

|  | Lap | Full | Queen |
|---|---|---|---|
| Size | 63½" x 77½" | 80½" x 94½" | 101½" x 115½" |
| Number of blocks | 12 | 20 | 30 |
| Block set | 3 x 4 | 4 x 5 | 5 x 6 |

## Materials:

*42"-wide fabric (40" of usable width after preshrinking and removing selvages)*

|  | Lap | Full | Queen |
|---|---|---|---|
| 5" background squares | 66 pairs | 102 pairs | 148 pairs |
| 5" dark squares | 66 pairs | 102 pairs | 148 pairs |
| Sashing | ⅝ yd. | 1 yd. | 1⅝ yds. |
| Inner and outer borders and binding | 2 yds. | 2⅝ yds. | 3⅝ yds. |
| Backing | 4 yds. | 5¾ yds. | 9 yds. |
| Batting | 68" x 82" | 85" x 99" | 106" x 120" |

## Cutting

*Cut all strips the width of the fabric.*

**Note:** Wait to cut the strips for the inner border until the quilt top is finished (see "Pieced Borders" on page 22).

| *Lap Size* | First Cut | | Second Cut | |
|---|---|---|---|---|
|  | Number of Strips | Strip Width | Number of Pieces | Piece Size |
| Sashing (vertical) | 4 | 2¼" | 8 strips 3 strips | 2¼" x 14½" 2¼" x 13" |
| Sashing (horizontal) | 3 | 2¼" | See directions for additional cutting. | |
| Inner border (sides) | 3 | 2¼" | | |
| Inner border (top and bottom) | 3 | 1⅜" | | |
| Outer border | 8 | 4" | | |
| Binding | 8 | 2½" | | |

| *Full Size* | First Cut | | Second Cut | |
|---|---|---|---|---|
|  | Number of Strips | Strip Width | Number of Pieces | Piece Size |
| Sashing (vertical) | 8 | 2" | 15 | 2" x 14½" |
| Sashing (horizontal) | 6 | 1¾" | See directions for additional cutting. | |
| Inner border (sides) | 4 | 1¾" | | |
| Inner border (top and bottom) | 4 | 1½" | | |
| Outer borders | 9 | 5½" | | |
| Binding | 10 | 2½" | | |

| Queen Size | First Cut | | Second Cut | |
|---|---|---|---|---|
| | Number of Strips | Strip Width | Number of Pieces | Piece Size |
| Sashing (vertical) | 12 | 2¼" | 24 | 2¼" x 14½" |
| Sashing (horizontal) | 10 | 2¼" | | |
| Inner border (sides) | 5 | 4" | | |
| Inner border (top and bottom) | 5 | 3⅛" | | |
| Outer borders | 10 | 5½" | | |
| Binding | 12 | 2½" | | |

## Making the Blocks

For each block you will need:
  4 pairs of 5" background squares
  4 pairs of 5" dark or medium squares

1. Referring to the directions for the "Small-Wonders Units" on page 16, make the components for the block. Use 1 pair of background and 1 pair of dark fabrics for each star block.

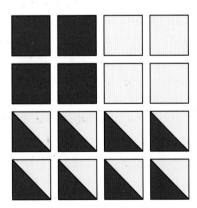

Small-wonders units

2. Arrange the small-wonders units in 4 horizontal rows. Sew together in rows and press the seams in opposite directions from row to row. Sew the small-wonders units together to form stars.

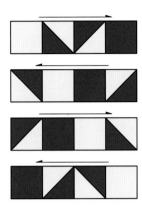

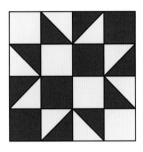

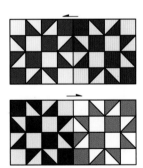

Make 4
for each block.

3. Sew 4 stars together to complete the block. Press.

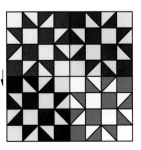

All That Glitters block

4. Follow steps 1–3 to make the required number of blocks for the quilt size you are making.

## Making the Pieced Border

*Pieced-Border Blocks*

|  | Lap | Full | Queen |
|---|---|---|---|
| Side | 9 per strip | 11 per strip | 14 per strip |
| Top and bottom | 7 per strip | 9 per strip | 12 per strip |
| Total border blocks | 32 | 40 | 52 |

1. For each Half-Star border block, you will need one 5" background square and one 5" dark square. Make small-wonders units following the directions on page 16.

2. Arrange the units from step 1 in 2 horizontal rows. Sew the units together in rows and press the seams in opposite directions from row to row. Sew the rows together to make the Half Star blocks. Make the required number of border blocks for your quilt.

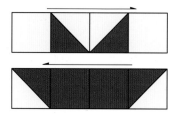

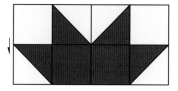

Half Star block

3. For each of the 4 corner blocks, make small-wonders units using 1 dark 5" square and 1 background 5" square. Arrange the units as shown in horizontal rows, sew together in rows, and press as directed. Sew the rows together to complete each corner block.

Make 4 corner blocks.

## Assembling the Quilt Top

1. For the lap-size quilt, sew a 2¼" x 13" strip to each of the three 2¼" x 40" horizontal sashing strips. For the full-size quilt, cut 2 of the sashing strips in half and sew 1 to each of the remaining 1¾" x 40" sashing strips. For the queen-size quilt, sew the 2¼" x 40" sashing strips together in pairs.

2. Referring to the quilt plan and working on your design wall, arrange the blocks with short, vertical sashing strips between the blocks. Sew the blocks and short sashing strips together in rows and press the seams toward the sashing strips.

3. Measure the completed block rows, average the measurements if they are not the same, and cut the required number of horizontal sashing strips for your quilt from the long sashing strips.

4. Sew the block rows together with sashing strips between them. Press the seams toward the sashing strips.

**Note:** There are no sashing strips at the top and bottom edges of this quilt top.

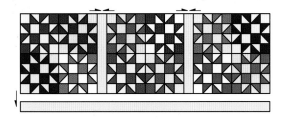

5. Referring to "Pieced Borders" on page 22, add the inner, pieced, and outer borders to quilt top.

## Finishing

1. Layer the quilt top with batting and backing; hand or machine baste the layers together (see page 23).

2. Quilt as desired, bind the edges, add a label, and enjoy your finished quilt.

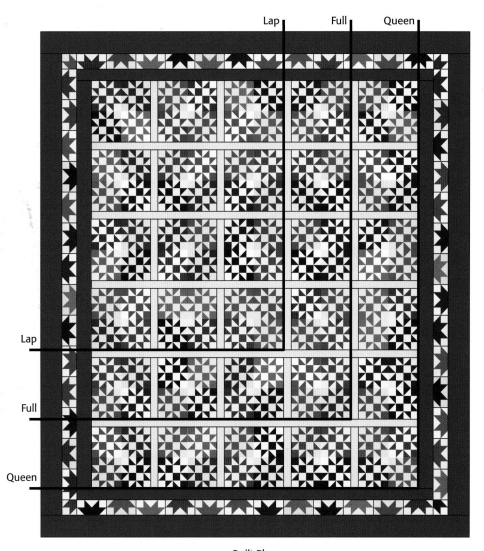

Quilt Plan

# ❧ Big Dipper ❧

*By Pat Speth, Davenport, Iowa, 1999, 81" x 106"*
*Finished block size: 7"*

*M*any of the dark squares in this diagonally set quilt came from a "Quilter's Choice" 5" fabric trade sponsored by our guild. If it was a 5" square of 100 percent cotton, you could trade it! For a calming effect, we chose the blue fabric for the setting triangles and sashing so the blocks appear as if they're floating in a blue, blue sky.

➻ *Skill level:* Intermediate

## Quilt Sizes and Statistics

|  | Lap | Full | Queen |
|---|---|---|---|
| Size | 68¾" x 68¾" | 81" x 106" | 106" x 106" |
| Number of blocks | 41 | 83 | 113 |
| Diagonal block set | 5 x 5 | 6 x 8 | 8 x 8 |

## Materials

*42"-wide fabric (40" of usable width after preshrinking and removing selvages)*

|  | Lap | Full | Queen |
|---|---|---|---|
| 5" dark squares | 41 pairs | 83 pairs | 113 pairs |
| 5" light squares | 41 pairs | 83 pairs | 113 pairs |
| Background, border, and binding | 3⅜ yds. | 5⅛ yds. | 6½ yds. |
| Backing | 4¼ yds. | 7⅜ yds. | 9½ yds. |
| Batting | 73" x 73" | 85" x 110" | 110" x 110" |

## Cutting

*Cut all strips across the fabric width (crosswise grain).*

### Lap Size

|  | First Cut | | Second Cut | |
|---|---|---|---|---|
|  | Number of Strips | Strip Width | Number of Pieces | Piece Size |
| Background | 2 | 13¾" | 4 | 13¾" x 13¾" |
|  |  |  | 2 | 7¼" x 7 ¼" |
|  | 7 | 2¼" | 34 | 2¼" x 7½" |
|  | 7 | 2¼" |  | See directions for additional cutting. |
| Border | 7 | 5" |  |  |
| Binding | 8 | 2½" |  |  |

### Full Size

|  | First Cut | | Second Cut | |
|---|---|---|---|---|
|  | Number of Strips | Strip Width | Number of Pieces | Piece Size |
| Background | 2 | 13¾" | 6 | 13¾" x 13¾" |
|  | 1 | 7¼" | 2 | 7¼" x 7¼" |
|  | 15 | 2¼" | 72 | 2¼" x 7½" |
|  | 15 | 2¼" |  | See directions for additional cutting. |
| Border | 9 | 5" |  |  |
| Binding | 10 | 2½" |  |  |

### Queen Size

|  | First Cut | | Second Cut | |
|---|---|---|---|---|
|  | Number of Strips | Strip Width | Number of Pieces | Piece Size |
| Background | 3 | 13¾" | 7 | 13¾" x 13¾" |
|  |  |  | 2 | 7¼" x 7¼" |
|  | 20 | 2¼" | 100 | 2¼" x 7½" |
|  | 23 | 2¼" |  | See directions for additional cutting. |
| Border | 11 | 5" |  |  |
| Binding | 12 | 2½" |  |  |

## Making the Blocks

For each block you will need:
    1 pair of 5" dark squares
    1 pair of 5" light squares

1. Referring to "Hourglass Units" on page 17 and using 1 pair each of dark and light squares, make 4 hourglass units for each block required.

2. Sew the hourglass units together in 2 horizontal rows for each block. Press seams in opposite directions. Sew the rows together to complete each block. Press.

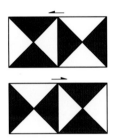
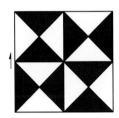

Big Dipper block

3. Follow steps 1 and 2 to make the required number of blocks for the quilt size you are making.

## Assembling the Quilt Top

1. Cut the 7¼" background squares in half on the diagonal to yield 4 corner triangles.

Corner triangles

2. Refer to the cutting chart for the number of 13¾" background squares for your quilt. Cut each one twice diagonally to yield 4 setting triangles per square.

Side setting triangles

3. Referring to the quilt plan and working on your design wall, arrange the blocks and the 2¼" x 7½" sashing strips in diagonal rows. Sew the blocks and sashing strips together in each row and press the seams toward the sashing strips.

4. Measure the lower edge of each completed block row to determine the required length for the sashing strip. Cut the required strips from the 2¼" x 40" sashing strips, piecing them if necessary. Sew sashing strips to the bottom edge of each row. Press the seams toward the sashing strips. Add setting triangles to the ends of each row and press the seams toward the setting triangles.

5. To sew the sashed rows together for all sizes, begin from the top left corner. Follow the quilt assembly diagram and directions below for the quilt size you are making.

**Lap size:** Sew together rows 1–3, 4–6, and 7–9 in 3 sections, leaving the upper right and lower left corner sections separate.

**Twin size:** Sew rows 1–7 and 8–13 together in 2 sections, leaving the upper right and lower left corner sections separate.

**Queen size:** Sew rows 1–6, 7–9, and 10–15 together in 3 sections, leaving the upper right and lower left corner sections separate.

Sew the large sections together and add the corner sections. Press all seams toward the sashing strips, setting triangles, and corner triangles.

6. The corner and side setting triangles were cut larger than needed and will extend beyond the block points. Use a ruler and rotary cutter to trim the excess at each edge of the quilt, leaving a ¼"-wide seam allowance beyond the block points.

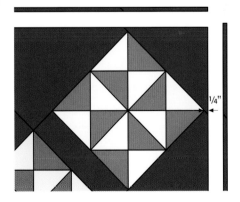

7. Add the borders, referring to "Plain Borders" on page 21.

# Finishing

1. Layer the quilt top with batting and backing; hand or machine baste the layers together (see page 23).
2. Quilt as desired, bind the edges, add a label, and enjoy your finished quilt.

Corner section

Full-Size Quilt Assembly Diagram

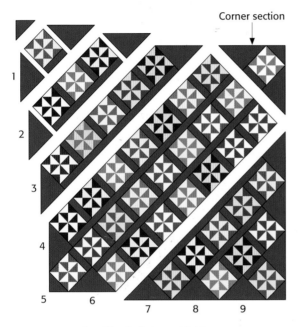

Corner section

Lap-Size Quilt Assembly Diagram

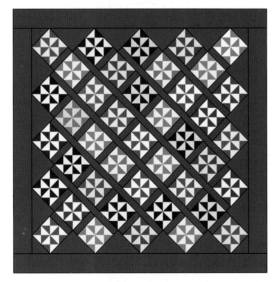

Lap-Size Quilt Plan

Full-Size Quilt Plan

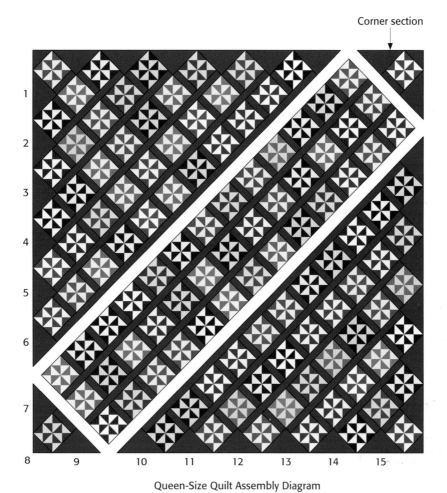

Queen-Size Quilt Assembly Diagram

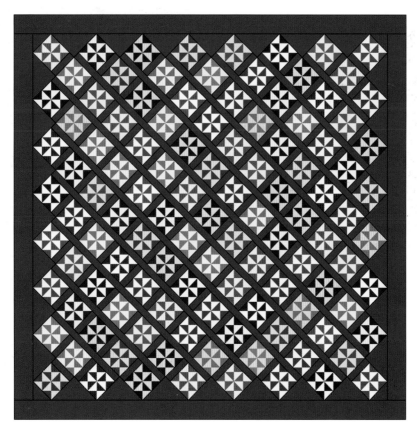

Queen-Size Quilt Plan

# ✳ *Arlington Square* ✳

*By Pat Speth, 2001, Davenport, Iowa, 76½" x 104½".*
*Finished block size: 14"*

*W*ith its bold mix of floral, tone-on-tone, geometric, and novelty prints, this dynamic quilt has a little bit of everything! An easy-to-stitch pieced border frames the blocks. Many different background fabrics enhance the finished appearance.

❧ *Skill level:* Intermediate

## Quilt Sizes and Statistics

|  | Lap | Twin | Queen |
|---|---|---|---|
| Size | 64½" x 64½" | 76½" x 104½" | 104½" x 104½" |
| Number of blocks | 9 | 24 | 36 |
| Block set | 3 x 3 | 4 x 6 | 6 x 6 |

## Materials

*42"-wide fabric (40" of usable width after preshrinking and removing selvages)*

|  | Lap | Twin | Queen |
|---|---|---|---|
| 5" light squares | 97 | 198 | 272 |
| 5" tone-on-tone squares | 9 sets of 3 | 24 sets of 3 | 36 sets of 3 |
| 5" dark squares | 94 | 215 | 309 |
| Borders and binding | 2⅛ yds. | 2⅝ yds. | 3 yds. |
| Backing | 4 yds. | 6¼ yds. | 9½ yds. |
| Batting | 69" x 69" | 81" x 109" | 109" x 109" |

## Cutting

*Cut all strips across the fabric width (crosswise grain).*
**Note:** Wait to cut the strips for the inner border until the quilt top is finished (refer to "Pieced Borders" on page 22).

*Lap Size*

|  | Number of Strips | Strip Width |
|---|---|---|
| Inner border | 6 | 3½" |
| Outer border | 7 | 4½" |
| Binding | 7 | 2½" |

*Twin Size*

|  | Number of Strips | Strip Width |
|---|---|---|
| Inner border | 8 | 2½" |
| Outer border | 9 | 4½" |
| Binding | 10 | 2½" |

*Queen Size*

|  | Number of Strips | Strip Width |
|---|---|---|
| Inner border | 10 | 2½" |
| Outer border | 10 | 4½" |
| Binding | 11 | 2½" |

## Making the Blocks

For each block you will need:
- 3 assorted light 5" squares for star points and picket-fence units
- 3 tone-on-tone 5" squares for block sashing
- Assorted 5" light and dark squares for four-patch units
- 4 assorted 5" squares for picket-fence units
- 2 assorted dark 5" squares. (You will cut these into smaller units to use in this block and successive blocks; see step 6 below.)

1. Cut each 5" light square into 2½" squares.

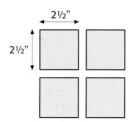

2. For each block, trim ½" from one edge of 2 tone-on-tone squares. In the opposite direction, cut each resulting rectangle into 2 rectangles, each 2½" x 4½", for a total of 4 rectangles. Cut the remaining tone-on-tone 5" square into 4 squares, each 2½" x 2½".

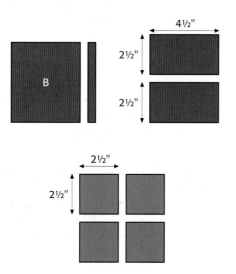

3. Select 4 different light 2½" squares and 1 set of 4 identical tone-on-tone 2½" squares to make the star points. Draw a diagonal line on the wrong side of the light 2½" squares. Stitch as directed and press toward the dark triangle. Stitch the waste triangles if desired.

Half-square-triangle unit

4. Referring to "Four-Patch Units" on page 14, and using assorted 5" squares, make 4 scrappy four-patch units for each block.

Make 4 for each block.

5. Referring to "Picket-Fence Units" on page 18, make 4 pairs of picket-fence units for each block.

**Note:** In the quilt shown, matched pairs of picket-fence units were used in each quarter of the block.

Make 4 pairs for each block.

6. Cut 2 dark 5" squares into four 2½" squares each. Use 5 for 1 block and set the remainder aside for future blocks.

7. Arrange the units in horizontal rows and sew together. Press in the direction of the arrows. Sew the rows together to complete each block. Press.

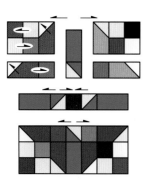

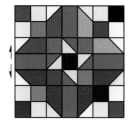

Arlington Square block

8. Follow steps 1–7 to make the required number of blocks for the quilt size you are making.

## Making the Pieced Border

*Pieced-Border Units*

|  | Lap | Twin | Queen |
| --- | --- | --- | --- |
| Side | 12 per strip | 22 per strip | 22 per strip |
| Top and bottom | 12 per strip | 15 per strip | 22 per strip |
| Total border units | 96 | 148 | 176 |
| Total border blocks | 48 | 74 | 88 |

1. Make picket-fence units, following the directions on page 18, but cut the 2½" x 4½" pieces from 5" light squares. Cut the 2½" squares from 5" dark squares. Sew the dark squares to the left side only of each rectangle, making the required number of border units for your quilt size (see chart at left).

Picket-fence
border unit

2. Sew border units together in pairs to make the required number of blocks for your quilt size.

Picket Fence
border block

3. Referring to "Half-Square-Triangle Units" on page 14, make 4 units for the border corner units.

Make 4
border corner units.

4. Referring to the chart at left, assemble the border strips. Add a border corner unit to each end of the top and bottom borders.

## Assembling the Quilt Top

1. Referring to the quilt plan, arrange the blocks on your design wall. Sew the blocks together in horizontal rows and press the seams in opposite directions from row to row. Sew the rows together and press.

2. Referring to "Pieced Borders" on page 22, add the inner, pieced, and outer borders to quilt top.

## Finishing

1. Layer your quilt top with batting and backing; hand or machine baste the layers together (see page 23).

2. Quilt as desired, bind the edges, add a label, and enjoy your finished quilt.

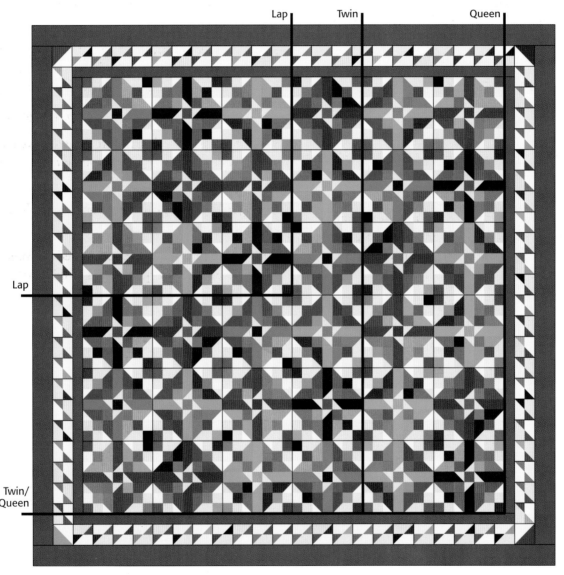

Quilt Plan

# Glossary

**Backing:** The bottom layer of the quilt; it covers the inner batting layer.

**Batting:** The middle layer of the quilt that provides warmth and thickness or "loft" to the quilt.

**Bias:** A (nasty) little four-letter word describing the 45° diagonal of fabric. Since this is the direction in which fabric stretches the most, it can cause problems for quiltmakers if not handled in the most respectful manner—that is to say, very carefully.

**Binding:** A separate strip of fabric used to enclose and finish the raw edges of all three layers of the quilt.

**Chain sewing:** Feeding consecutive sets of unit or block pieces under the presser foot in a continuous operation without clipping the threads in between as you go. It saves time and thread.

**Crosswise grain:** The woven threads that run perpendicular to the selvages. The crosswise grain has slightly more give and stretch than the lengthwise grain of fabric.

**Grain lines:** The vertical and horizontal orientation of the crosswise and lengthwise threads in a woven fabric.

**Ironing:** The act of pushing an iron across fabric yardage to remove the wrinkles prior to cutting.

**Lengthwise grain:** The threads that run parallel to the selvages (the length) in a woven fabric and have the least amount of stretch or give.

**Piecing:** The process of sewing together fabric pieces to make the blocks and assemble them into a quilt top.

**Pressing:** Setting the iron on a seam and pressing down (lightly) on the iron, and then lifting the iron and moving to the next spot and pressing down again.

**Quilt top:** The pieced or top layer of the quilt.

**Quilting:** The stitching used to hold all three layers of the quilt together. Quilting can be done either by hand or machine.

**Selvages:** The finished edges running the length of the fabric yardage.

**Unit:** One of the eight different pieced combinations used to construct the quilt blocks in this book.

# ❧ *About the Authors* ❧

*Charlene Thode, left, and Pat Speth*

Pat Speth and Charlene Thode live just a few blocks from each other in Davenport, Iowa. Even though their kids go to school together, they didn't actually meet until 1993—in their local quilt guild. Charlene had been a member since the mid-1980s and met Pat when she joined in 1993. Since then, the duo has organized guild quilt retreats and taught workshops. They agree that they're happiest when quilting and planning road trips together to buy fabric.

Pat started quilting in 1989 after purchasing wool quilt battings at her grandmother's auction. Charlene's grandmother introduced her to sewing and quilting by entertaining her with mail-order suit samples and then with cross-stitch blocks when she was just nine years old. She was reintroduced to quilting in the early 1980s. Pat and Charlene share

other interests as well—antiques, collectibles, and costume jewelry—and neither of them would know how to survive without a cat (or two) in the house.

Pat and her husband, Dan, have a son, Ray, in college and a daughter, Roxie, in high school. When she's not quilting, Pat works as the office manager of a dental office. Charlene shares her life with her husband, Arnie, and three children. Matt and Michelle are in college and Mike is in high school. Charlene works as a legal assistant.

Every day Pat and Charlene find they have more and more in common. Since they'll both be empty nesters at the same time, they've promised to spend the first few days together after the last of the kids are gone...quilting, of course!